To Tim O'Shea

With Best Wishes

Christy Brins

# THE LAIRDS OF ARBUTHNOTT

## Christy Bing

**Drawings**
**by**
**Clare Arbuthnott**

Reprinted and published in 1999 with minor alterations by
Agnate Press
34 Church Street, Edzell, Angus DD9 7TQ

© Christy Bing 1993 and 1999

First published in 1993 by Capability Publishing

Printed in Scotland by Halcon Printing Limited, Stonehaven

Designed by Pablo Thorley

A CIP catalogue record for this book is available from the British Library

ISBN 0 9535923 0 8

Every reasonable effort has been made to ensure that the information contained in this book is accurate and not misleading. The publishers, author and the Arbuthnott Family Association accept no responsibility for any errors or omissions.

*The Kirk of St Ternan, Arbuthnott around 1885. The Arbuthnott Aisle built by Robert, 12th Laird in the 1480s projects towards the trees. To the left is the schoolhouse which was on this site for about 200 years.*

# Foreword

*by*

*The Viscount of Arbuthnott,*

*KT CBE DSC MA FRSE*

As present Chief of the Name of Arbuthnott, I am constantly aware of my role in carrying on the traditions of the family. One of these has been to keep a record of events within the family as the years go by. Although Mrs P S-M Arbuthnot wrote in detail about the Aberdeenshire branch in 1920, she had very little access to information about the Kincardineshire Arbuthnotts. There has not been a proper history of the senior branch of the Arbuthnotts since around 1667, so the time is ripe for an update. My sister, Christy Bing, has put matters right and given the Lairds of Arbuthnott their due at last. I hope you will like what she has done as much as I do.

There are now Arbuthnot(t)s all over the world. It has been my pleasure to host a gathering attended by family members from as far away as America, Australia and New Zealand in 1977 and again in 1992. The overwhelming impression left by both events was of an extraordinary friendliness and good-will. It is my belief that all who read this book will be aware that the roots of that fellowship lie in our long shared history. The story, like all long stories, has moments of greatness and moments of obscurity, but in 800 years of history I hope you will find at least one of my forebears interesting.

# About the Author

Christy Bing was born Christian Keith Arbuthnott and is the sister of the present Viscount of Arbuthnott.

A graduate of Edinburgh University, she has been the family historian since 1977 and has devoted considerable time and energy to researching the history of the Arbuthnotts. Discovering several previously unrecorded events in the lives of her ancestors led her to an enthusiasm for the history of Scotland from which this book has sprung.

She now lives in Edzell, just down the road from the family home at Arbuthnott, with her husband, Peter. She has three sons, a daughter and a growing number of grandchildren.

## Colour Plates

# *Contents*

# Appendices

# *Chronology*

| SCOTLAND | | ARBUTHNOTT | |
|---|---|---|---|
| 600-400 BC | Arrival of Celts | | |
| 81 AD | Roman invasion | | |
| 563 | Arrival of Columba at Iona | | |
| 794 | First Viking attacks | | |
| 843 | Defeat of Picts by Kenneth MacAlpine | | |
| 1057-93 | Reign of Malcolm Canmore | | |
| 1124-53 | Reign of David I | | |
| 1165-1214 | Reign of William the Lion | 1170-1174 | Osbert Oliphant granted lands of Arbuthnott |
| 1189 | Third Crusade | c.1190-c.1200 | Hugh, 1st Laird of Arbuthnott |
| 1192 | Scottish Church becomes Pope's 'special daughter' | | |
| | | c.1200-c.1240 | Duncan, 2nd Laird |
| 1214-49 | Reign of Alexander II | 1206 | Synod at Perth, judgement against Duncan |
| 1249-86 | Reign of Alexander III | | |
| 1286-90 | Reign of Margaret 'Maid of Norway' | c.1240-c.1260 | Hugh, 3rd Laird |
| | | 1242 | Rededication of Arbuthnott Kirk |
| 1291-96 | Reign of John Balliol | | |
| 1296 | Edward I of England invades Scotland | c.1260-c.1300 | Hugh le Blond, 4th Laird |
| 1297-1305 | William Wallace leads fight against Edward I | c.1300-1314 | Duncan, 5th Laird |
| 1306-29 | Reign of Robert I (the Bruce) | | |
| 1314 | Battle of Bannockburn | 1314-c.1320 | Duncan, 6th Laird |
| 1329-71 | Reign of David II | c.1320-c.1350 | Hugh, 7th Laird |
| 1341 | Inverbervie created Royal Burgh | | |
| 1349-50 | First outbreak of Black Death | c.1350-c.1400 | Philip, 8th Laird |
| 1361 | Second outbreak of Black Death | | |
| 1371-90 | Reign of Robert II (the Steward) | | |
| | | 1372 | Philip, 8th Laird's marriage to Margaret Douglas |
| 1390-1406 | Reign of Robert III | | |
| 1406-37 | Reign of James I | c.1400-1446 | Hugh, 9th Laird |
| 1406-24 | James I held hostage in England | | |
| 1437 | James I murdered | 1420 | Murder of Sheriff Melville |
| 1437-60 | Reign of James II | | |

| | |
|---|---|
| 1460 | James II killed by bursting canon |
| 1460-1488 | Reign of James III |
| 1488 | Battle of Sauchieburn |
| 1488-1513 | Reign of James IV |
| 1503 | Marriage of James IV to Margaret Tudor |
| 1513 | Battle of Flodden |
| 1513-1542 | Reign of James V |
| 1542-67 | Reign of Mary, Queen of Scots |
| 1544-5 | 'Rough Wooing' |
| 1546 | Murder of Cardinal Beaton |
| 1567-1625 | Reign of James VI (later I of England) |
| 1603 | Union of Crowns |
| 1625-49 | Reign of Charles I |
| 1638 | National Covenant |
| 1647 | The Engagement |
| 1649 | Execution of Charles I |
| 1651-58 | Protectorate of Cromwell |
| 1660 | Restoration of the Monarchy |
| 1660-1685 | Reign of Charles II |
| 1685-88 | Reign of James VII & II |
| 1688 | The Glorious Revolution |
| 1689-1702 | Reign of William and Mary |

| | |
|---|---|
| 1446-1450 | Robert, 10th Laird |
| 1450-1470 | David, 11th Laird |
| 1470-1506 | Robert, 12th Laird |
| 1471 | James Sibbald appointed minister at Arbuthnott |
| 1475 | Robert,12th Laird marries Marion Scrymgeour |
| 1482 | Arbuthnott Psalter completed |
| 1482-3 | Arbuthnott Prayer book completed |
| 1484 | Death of Hugh at Brechin school |
| 1491 | Arbuthnott Missal completed |
| 1506-1521 | James,13th Laird |
| 1507 | James, 13th Laird married Lady Jean Stewart |
| 1520 | Licence to travel on pilgrimage |
| 1521-79 | Robert, 14th Laird |
| 1526 | Robert, 14th Laird marries Katherine Erskine |
| 1545 | Robert, 14th Laird granted kirklands |
| 1579-1606 | Andrew, 15th Laird |
| 1583 | Death of Principal Arbuthnott |
| 1606-31 | Robert, 16th Laird |
| 1631-33 | Robert, 17th Laird |
| 1633-55 | Robert, 1st Viscount/18th Laird |
| 1641 | Charles I creates Viscountcy of Arbuthnott |
| 1645 | Arbuthnott laid waste by Montrose's army |
| 1655-82 | Robert, 2nd Viscount/19th Laird |
| 1681 | 2nd Viscount takes Test |
| 1682-94 | Robert, 3rd Viscount/20th Laird |
| 1683 | 3rd Viscount marries Lady Ann Gordon |
| 1694-1710 | Robert, 4th Viscount/21st Laird |

| | | | | |
|---|---|---|---|---|
| 1702-1714 | Reign of Anne | | 1710-56 | John, 5th Viscount/22nd Laird |
| 1707 | Act of Union | | 1715 | Sale of Arrat to fund Jacobite cause |
| 1714-27 | Reign of George I | | | |
| 1715 | 1st Jacobite Rising Battle of Sheriffmuir | | 1754 | Contract for rebuilding of Arbuthnott House |
| 1727-60 | Reign of George II | | | |
| 1745 | 2nd Jacobite Rising | | 1756-91 | John, 6th Viscount/23rd Laird |
| 1746 | Battle of Culloden | | 1791-1800 | John, 7th Viscount/24th Laird |
| 1760-1820 | Reign of George III | | 1792 | Building of Home Farm steading |
| | | | 1794 | Survey of Arbuthnott parish |
| | | | 1800-60 | John, 8th Viscount/25th Laird |
| 1820-30 | Reign of George IV | | 1829 | 8th Viscount sustains fractured skull |
| 1830-37 | Reign of William IV | | 1843 | Second survey of Arbuthnott parish |
| 1837-1901 | Reign of Victoria | | 1848 | 8th Viscount charged with forgery |
| | | | 1860-91 | John, 9th Viscount/26th Laird |
| | | | 1891-95 | John, 10th Viscount/27th Laird |
| | | | 1895-1912 | David, 11th Viscount/28th Laird |
| 1901 -1911 | Reign of Edward VII | | 1912-17 | William, 12th Viscount/29th Laird |
| 1911-1935 | Reign of George V | | 1917-20 | Walter, 13th Viscount/30th Laird |
| 1914-18 | 1st World War | | 1920-60 | John, 14th Viscount/31st Laird |
| 1935-36 | Reign of Edward VIII | | 1960-66 | Robert, 15th Viscount/32nd Laird |
| 1936-52 | Reign of George VI | | 1966- | John,16th Viscount/33rd Laird |
| 1939-45 | 2nd World War | | 1986-87 | John, 16th Viscount appointed Lord High Commissioner to Church of Scotland |
| 1952- | Reign of Elizabeth II | | 1996 | John 16th Viscount appointed Knight of the Thistle |

# Introduction

In 1977, prior to the first family gathering at Arbuthnott, I wrote a short history called The Family of Arbuthnott. I undertook this at the request of my brother, the present Laird of Arbuthnott. The idea was inspired by the many letters received from all corners of the globe which came as an enthusiastic endorsement of the idea that a family association should be started. These letters showed that some Arbuthnotts did not know of their Scottish origins, indeed they believed their roots lay in Ireland. So in it I showed how anyone called Arbuthnott or Arbuthnot can be sure that their ancestors came from one specific area of Scotland. I did this by relating how members of the family had moved from the place called Arbuthnott on the east coast of Scotland. Firstly some moved to Aberdeenshire and Edinburgh and some to France, then many, particularly in the seventeenth century, went to Ireland and thence to the United States and Canada, later still to South Africa, Australia and New Zealand.

Since then the Arbuthnott Family Association has held many gatherings worldwide, finding a feeling of identification and empathy through the knowledge of a shared family heritage. Arbuthnotts know about their roots on the east coast of Scotland, whether they end the spelling with one "t" or two (at one time the Lairds of Arbuthnott happily spelt it both ways within the same document). They know of each other and have corresponded and worked out their family trees, with the meticulous and painstaking help of William Arbuthnot, our family genealogist. In the United States, in particular, Mrs Margaret Ridall has completed an enormous task in publishing an American genealogy, prefaced by a specially adapted version of my original history.

As family historian, I have been asked to write another history of the family. To those who may think I have taken a long time over it, I have to say that it has been a lengthy task, and I have still not researched nearly enough for my own satisfaction and am only too conscious of its omissions and inadequacies.

Firstly, I feel I have not done justice to the Ladies of Arbuthnott. The Lairds have, with but one or two exceptions, chosen worthy helpmeets. If I can take my own mother, the wife of the fifteenth Viscount, as an example, here was someone who was constantly encouraging and caring for her husband and was completely selfless in her support. The fact that she hardly features at all in the account of her husband's career would have met with her unqualified approval.

Secondly, I found that I could not tell the story of the Arbuthnotts without relating it to the background of Scottish history in general, so to those who, like Henry Ford, think that *"history is bunk"* or more simply just boring (I have not had to look too far for one with that opinion), let me say that this history would have had little meaning without an account of the times contemporary with each Laird. I have in general tried to start each chapter with the national history of the times before recounting events at Arbuthnott and, in the case of the Kings of Scotland after the Union of the Crowns, I have referred to them with the Scots title first, thus James VI and I.

1

Thirdly, I have confined my story almost entirely to that of the Lairds themselves. The book is a celebration of the fact that when in 1977 and 1992 Arbuthnotts gathered together in Scotland from many distant lands, they could still meet at our family home and be greeted by the direct descendant of Hugh de Swinton who came to the lands then called Aberbothenoth around 1185. Since that time thirty-three Lairds have succeeded one another in the direct male line, living on the same site and farming the same lands for over eight hundred years.

There have been other family chroniclers. Four hundred years ago Alexander Arbuthnott, grandson of the twelfth Laird, Principal of Kings College, Aberdeen wrote the first family history in Latin, his text was translated or 'englifchit' by M. V. Morison, parson of Benholm. This history was continued a hundred years later by the Reverend Alexander Arbuthnot, rector at Arbuthnott. (In the book I refer to the first Alexander always as Principal Arbuthnott, even before he had actually earned that title, to avoid confusing him with the second, Reverend, Alexander.) Then in 1920 Mrs P S-M Arbuthnot published her *Memories of the Arbuthnots of Kincardineshire and Aberdeenshire,* I commend it to any descendants of the Aberdeenshire branch. Finally, ten years ago, came Harry Gordon Slade's study *Arbuthnott House.* I follow these predecessors with respect and thanks, particularly to Principal Arbuthnott to whom the Arbuthnott family owes immeasurable gratitude.

### Acknowledgements

My thanks are due to Colin MacLaren, Ian Beavan and the staff of the Department of Special Collections and Archives at the University of Aberdeen; to Norman Atkinson, Rachel Benvie and Mary Cook of Montrose Museum; to Paisley Museum for permission to reproduce the portrait of St Ternan from the Arbuthnott Missal and to the Imperial War Museum for the photograph of my father; to Margaret Florence of Edzell for her kind help and the use of her Scottish National Dictionaries; to John Mann of Broughty Ferry for his research on the 8th Viscount; to Richard Siwek, David Clark and David Darling, photographers.

Also, my thanks to all my family who have supported me in their various ways; the Laird himself; Keith, my computer consultant; Clare, whose drawings grace my text; my cousin, Meg Blair-Imrie and her excellent memory; the family proof readers, particularly my son Robert, whose comments and support have been so valuable; but mostly my thanks to Sarah, my daughter-in-law, who is my editor and adviser and without whose expertise this book would never have taken the form it has. Special thanks to my long-suffering husband, Peter, whose patience has been stretched to the full and who has learnt to work the microwave during the preparation of this book.

Christy Bing
February 1993

# THE LAIRDS OF ARBUTHNOTT

**Hugh de Swinton**, 1st Laird of Arbuthnott, c.1190–c.1200

**Duncan de Aberbothenoth**, 2nd Laird, c.1200–c.1240

**Hugh de Aberbothenoth**, 3rd Laird, c.1240–c.1260

**Hugh le Blond**, 4th Laird, c.1260–c.1300

**Duncan de Aberbothenoth**, 5th Laird, c.1300–1314

**Duncan de Aberbothenoth**, 6th Laird, 1314–c.1320

**Hugh de Arbuthnott**, 7th Laird, c.1320–c.1350

**Philip de Arbuthnott**, 8th Laird, c.1350–c.1400 =1. Lady Janet Keith =2. Margaret Douglas of Dalkeith

**Hugh Arbuthnott**, 9th Laird, c.1400–1446 = Lady Margaret Keith

**Robert Arbuthnott**, 10th Laird, 1446-50 = Giles Ogilvy of Lintrathen

**David Arbuthnott**, 11th Laird, 1450-70 = Elizabeth Durham of Grange

**Sir Robert Arbuthnott**, 12th Laird, 1470-1506 =1. Margaret Wishart of Pitarrow =2. Marion Scrymgeour of Dudhope

**James Arbuthnott**, 13th Laird, 1506-21 = Lady Jean Stewart

**Robert Arbuthnott**, 14th Laird, 1521-79 =1. Katherine Erskine of Dun =2. Lady Christian Keith = 3. Helen Clephane

**Andrew Arbuthnott**, 15th Laird, 1579-1606 =1. Lady Elizabeth Carnegie =2. Margaret Hoppringal

**James Arbuthnott of Arrat**, d.1606 = Margaret Livingstone of Dunipace

**Sir Robert Arbuthnott**, 16th Laird, 1606-31 = Lady Mary Keith

**James Arbuthnott** =1. Lady Margaret Keith =2. Margaret Fraser

**Sir Robert Arbuthnott**, 17th Laird, 1631-33

**Sir Robert Arbuthnott**, 1st Viscount and 18th Laird, 1633-55

3

# THE VISCOUNTS OF ARBUTHNOTT

**Robert Arbuthnott** =1. Lady Marjorie Carnegie =2. Katherine Fraser
1st Viscount, 1633-55

**Robert Arbuthnott** =1. Lady Elizabeth Keith =2. Katherine Gordon of Pitlurg & Straloch
2nd Viscount, 1655-82

**John Arbuthnott** of Fordoun = Margaret Falconer of Phesdo
d. 1737

**John Arbuthnott** = 1. Mary Douglas =2. Jean Arbuthnott
6th Viscount, 1756-91 of Bridgeford of Findowrie

**Robert Arbuthnott** = Lady Anne Gordon
3rd Viscount, 1682-94

**Robert Arbuthnott** **John Arbuthnott** = Jean Morrison of Prestongrange
4th Viscount, 1694-1710 5th Viscount, 1710-56

**John Arbuthnott** = Isabella Graham of Morphie
7th Viscount, 1791-1800

**John Arbuthnott** = Margaret Ogilvy of Clova
8th Viscount, 1800-60

**Hugh Arbuthnott** = Susannah Campbell
d.1866

**John Arbuthnott** = Jeannie Hamilton
d.1923

**John Arbuthnott** = Lady Jean Ogilvy
9th Viscount, 1860-91

**Walter Arbuthnott** = Ann Otley of Delaford
d. 1891

**Walter Arbuthnott** = Marion Parlby
13th Viscount, of Manadon
1917-20

**Robert Keith Arbuthnott** = Ursula Collingwood
15th Viscount, 1960-66 of Dedham

**John Arbuthnott** = Harriet Allen **David Arbuthnott**
10th Viscount, of Inchmartin 11th Viscount,
1891-95 1895-1912

**William Arbuthnott**
12th Viscount,
1912-17

**John Arbuthnott** = Dorothy Oxley of Ripon
14th Viscount, 1920-60

**John Arbuthnott** = Mary Oxley
16th Viscount, 1966- of Morley

**Keith Arbuthnott** = Jilly Farquharson of Whitehouse
Master of Arbuthnott

Clare      Christopher      Rachel

4

Highlands

Banchory ● ● Aberdeen

● Stonehaven

Fettercairn ● ● Arbuthnott

Brechin ● ● Montrose

HIGHLAND LINE

● St Andrews

● Edinburgh

Lowlands

Ireland

# SCOTLAND

5

# Chapter 1

## Whence We Came

The story of the Arbuthnott family runs like a thread woven into the fabric of the long history of Scotland. To set a background to that history, it is important to look at the character of the countryside which has had such an overwhelming influence on the history of the Scots.

The map of Scotland shows a country of strong contrasts. To the west, a jagged coastline of small islands and long sea lochs borders a very large area of mountains. These are the highlands, they represent the Scotland of the romantic image; of soft mists, heather-clad hills and grazing sheep. The land there is beautiful, but unproductive. It is also inaccessible. Until Bonnie Prince Charlie's failed rebellion in 1745, invaders never managed to tame the Highlanders, whose mountains always gave them protection.

The highlands are divided from the lowlands by the 'Highland Line', a massive geological fault running diagonally across the country. It starts at the mouth of the river Clyde in the west and ends in the foothills of the Grampians near Stonehaven in the north east. The lowland coast is sharply defined, but with many good natural harbours and the countryside is either flat or gently rolling. As a result the Lowlander has always been subjected to waves of invaders who, over thousands of years, have come, usually by sea, in search of fertile lands on which to settle. It is with the fortunes of these Lowland Scots that this story is concerned.

### The Place called Arbuthnott

The contrast between the highlands and lowlands is well illustrated when crossing over the northern end of the Highland Line on the road from Banchory to Fettercairn. First the road passes through typical highland scenery of larch and pine woodland. Later it crosses a bridge over a burn which, springing from high in the hills, runs down through a small valley. There sheep graze on the coarse grass and the occasional birch or rowan tree leans away from the prevailing wind. In a sheltered spot stand the ruins of a croft. Then the road leads on to higher ground where hills covered in heather spread up and out to the horizon.

At the Cairn o'Mount, it reaches its highest point, and suddenly the view opens out. Far below are the green fertile lands of the Howe of the Mearns, which lie at the northern end of Strathmore. Ahead to the south-east, on a clear day, the harbour town of Montrose can be seen silhouetted against the sea. Panning left, the low Hill of Garvock runs northwards. The view is then interrupted by the higher Strathfinella Hill. When it opens out again the sea can be seen once more shimmering in the far distance. Three miles inland from that shore, tucked in the valley of a small river called the Bervie Water, are the lands of Arbuthnott.

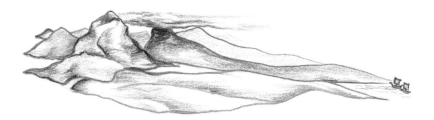

*The highland-lowland landscape of Scotland*

The Bervie Water, born of four small burns, starts on its short, winding journey to the sea in the hills a few miles over to the north. First it runs down through Glenbervie, then bends and twists across the plain, and at Kair, near Fordoun, it heads down towards the sea. Further on, after the ground starts to rise steeply on either side, the sloping lawns of a garden come into view through the trees on the north side, and above them stands Arbuthnott House. Here a small burn runs down into the river. This burn was called Bothenoth or 'little stream of virtue' in ancient times, because it was thought to hold special powers of healing. The lands where it joins the Bervie Water were called Aberbothenoth, the name which later became Arbuthnott. After another sharp bend the river flows past the ancient kirk of Arbuthnott, skirting the hillock known as the Viking Mound, near which stand the ruins of the millhouse and the mill. Further on, having passed the Castle of Allardice, the river finally reaches the sea at the small town of Inverbervie.

The landscape has changed remarkably little at Arbuthnott over the centuries. If the founder of the family, Hugh de Swinton, were to return after eight hundred years, he would easily recognise the same landmarks. Arbuthnott House is on the spot where he once lived, and the kirk still stands in the same place, but the numerous small communities which lived on the kirklands and elsewhere have gone. In Hugh's day the population of Scotland, although smaller, was spread out much more evenly over the countryside than it is today.

The low-lying fields which were then mostly marshes are now cultivated. This transformation in the condition of the land was brought about by the big river embankment and drainage schemes which were started at the end of the eighteenth century, in a period that saw many ambitious land improvements as the Agricultural Revolution took hold in Scotland. When this task was undertaken workmen dug up two skeletons of prehistoric deer. Their antlers have been preserved at Arbuthnott and take us back to a time long before the first men ever reached Scotland.

### Earliest Times

These antlers come from the outsize forebears of a species of deer, probably elk, which roamed in the forests then covering the land over 10,000 years ago. Another two thousand years were to pass before the first men reached the area. These people came in small nomadic groups of hunters and food-gatherers. They travelled across what is now the North Sea  but which was then still a part of the European land mass. They too lived in the forests, hunting for meat and fishing in the river, always on the move because they had not yet learnt the art of growing crops or domesticating animals.

The breakthrough came around 4,000 BC when the first farmers arrived. They originally came from western Asia and travelled through Europe, pushing ever further on in search of good, fertile land. This was the first time that men settled at Arbuthnott and started to cultivate the higher ground. These people were still of the Stone Age and had only crude tools. Their flint knives have been dug up in Arbuthnott parish.

By around 2,000 BC implements had improved. It was about this time that the Bronze Age reached Arbuthnott and with it a gradually increasing skill in the craft of metal work. The art came both through the evolution of old skills and by learning from new settlers. The first people who used these tools were called the Beaker Folk, because of the distinctive style of the pottery found in their graves. They placed their dead in small stone coffins with the body in a crouched position, often with a pottery vessel which held either food, a weapon, even a necklace for the after-life. Such a grave was found at Arbuthnott in the nineteenth century, but the skeleton and contents crumbled to dust on exposure to the air. Another dramatic legacy from the distant past which can still be seen are the standing stones found near Arbuthnott. They remain arresting symbols of a forgotten form of worship.

### The Celts and Romans

The Iron Age brought in the next stage of development around 600-400 BC with the arrival of the first of the Celtic settlers. They came from the Continent and this time left more structured evidence of their way of life. (None is any longer discernible at Arbuthnott, but some pre-historic dwellings were unearthed in the nineteenth century. They caused little excitement at the time and were ploughed into the ground.) They built their homesteads in the form of circular huts, with farm steadings for their livestock and for storing grain. The Celts built hill-forts, surrounded by ditches and ramparts and were to remain the dominant race for many centuries. They were divided into many groups and tribes; those on the east coast were part of a large tribe called the Caledonians, who were to feature in the next drama to affect the lowlands.

This was the Roman invasion, an account of which appears in the first written history of Scotland, or Caledonia as it was then called. The author was Tacitus, nephew of Agricola under whose command the Roman 9th Legion marched northwards in 81 AD. The Romans intended to conquer Scotland having already subdued most of England. Supported by their ships from the sea, they were the first people to launch a major military invasion by land. By 84 AD they had managed to reach as far as north eastern Scotland, where they met and defeated the Caledonians at Mons Graupius, the exact site of which has never been established. They then advanced as far north as Forres, building fortified sites as they went. The land and the people proved too hostile and lines of communication too tenuous to maintain and so they were ordered to retreat.

Pursued and harried by the northern tribes after they had retreated, the Romans were forced to build a wall to protect their settlements. A wall which went from the Irish Sea to the North Sea across Cumbria and Northumberland, and was named after the Emperor Hadrian who was in Britain in 121 AD. This gave the Romans a firm base from which to push forward again and by 139 AD they were building the Antonine Wall across the Caledonian midland valley to the north.

The next time they came as far north as Arbuthnott was between 208 and 211 AD, when the legions under the Emperor Severus marched north occupying the sites that Agricola had built. Certainly one fort was Raedykes, west of Stonehaven but evidence of another has been found at Kair, two miles upstream from Arbuthnott. Severus remained in the north for three years but was finally worn out by continuous resistance from the native tribes. He retreated back behind Hadrian's Wall, dying soon after at York. The Romans never returned.

### The Picts and Scots

The Romans stayed only a brief time. The Picts, who were of Celtic stock and came originally from the European mainland, were dominant in eastern Scotland for possibly a thousand years. In 685, they defeated an invasion force from Northumbria at the Battle of Dunnichen. Remarkably little is known about them since their written language has baffled all experts. Among the only legacies that are identifiable as Pictish are carved stones, like those at Aberlemno in Angus, and many local place names. At Arbuthnott, the names Pitcarles and Pitforthie are Pictish.

Meanwhile across on the west side of Scotland another group of Celts, called the Scots, had come across the sea from Ireland. Until many centuries later when the marshes were drained and a good road system was built, journeys over land were extremely hazardous and travelling by water was far easier. Communications between one side of Scotland and the other were bad, whereas those between Ireland and Western Scotland were very close. Indeed the same royal dynasty ruled in both regions, both known as the Kingdom of Dalriada. For several centuries the land was divided with the Picts ruling in the east and the Scots in the west.

This situation remained until in the year 794, when the dreaded scourge of the Viking or Norse raiders came to the people. These fierce Scandinavian warriors were to terrify coastal dwellers, who would learn to flee from the sight of the long boats with their dragon shaped prows and the blonde men with their horned headgear. The Norsemen established colonies along the north and west coasts, eventually coming to terms with the local people, and strongly influencing events in Scotland for five hundred years. The Picts were so weakened by these raids that in 843, they were defeated by the Scots under Kenneth MacAlpine. The Scots now reigned supreme and this is how the country came, eventually, to be known as Scotland.

Although relations between the Scots and the Norsemen became peaceful, stories of raids by Vikings had entered the folklore of the people. One of the romantic tales told of Hugh le Blond, fourth Laird of Arbuthnott, was that he slew a dragon in the Den of Pitcarles. The dragon may well have represented a Viking chief as a dragon-prowed longboat could have launched an attack as far up the Bervie Water as Arbuthnott. The hillock below the kirk was long thought to be the burial mound of such a boat.

### The Celtic Church

The conquest by the Scots from Ireland was not only secular, it was also religious. Christianity was brought over by missionary monks, who were formidable men, being expert sailors as well as preachers and scholars. They carried the Gospel message as far as Iceland. One of the first was St Ninian but the best known of them all was St. Columba. A member of the Irish royal family, he had reputedly refused a kingdom in favour of taking the Christian message to the heathen. Among his many gifts was the art of illuminating and writing the scriptures. He founded the monastery and abbey at Iona, making it the centre from which monks went out to preach.

Columba, through his royal blood, was often related to the rulers he converted. Once a leader was won over, all the people were bound to follow. The Druids who had dominated Celtic hearts and minds were now driven out. Wherever he founded a church, St Columba left one of his illuminated scriptures. He died in 579 and was buried at Iona, which then became the burial place for all Scottish kings until, nearly three hundred years later, Kenneth MacAlpine carried the remains of St Columba to Dunkeld after his victory over the Picts.

Columba never reached the people of the Mearns. The man credited with their conversion to Christianity is St. Ternan, patron saint of the Kirk of Arbuthnott. It is difficult to separate fact from fiction in the story of St. Ternan. By the late middle ages a legend had grown up round him, most of which suited the church politics of the time. It affirmed that St Ternan, who was born of noble parents in the province of Myrnia (the Mearns), was converted to Christianity by St Palladius. He was then sent to Rome where he was instructed for seven years by Pope Gregory the Great. He returned to his native land with a miraculous bell. There he preached and converted the people. He became High Bishop of the Picts and was buried on an island in a loch near Banchory. His relics were kept in a local kirk there. This version of the life of St Ternan would put him in the fifth century, since Palladius* died at Fordoun around 424. However no evidence of a Christian burial has been found in the district of the Mearns earlier than the seventh century. It has to be remembered that the Celtic Church had grown up independently of Rome with Ireland, not the Papacy, as its inspiration.

The truth is that St. Ternan most probably lived sometime during the late sixth or seventh century, a native of the Mearns. He was possibly the first person to convert these, his own people, to the Christian faith. He may well have travelled to Ireland, either for training or to take up an appointment. He features in the Irish saint's calendar and there are records of a 'Terenan' as Bishop of Leinster. He had a saint's day dedicated to him on 12 June. He may have personally set up a church at Arbuthnott or it may have been dedicated to his memory.

## Late Celtic Times

After Kenneth MacAlpine conquered the Picts, kings in Scotland struggled to keep control of the country. The Norsemen held sway not only over Shetland, Orkney and the Western Isles but also large areas of Caithness and Sutherland. Dominion over large areas such as Lothian and Strathclyde in the south were continually disputed by kings and the powerful local nobles. An added menace was the incursions of the Anglo-Saxons from north Germany. Starting around the time of the Roman withdrawal, the Saxons gradually gained power in England, but never managed to establish a foothold north of the Forth. King Athelstan apparently reached "*Fordun*" in 937, perhaps coming up the Bervie valley during his foray.

Few kings died in their beds. It was necessary for a king to be physically capable of leading his subjects in battle. When he showed signs of weakness, he was usurped and either killed or blinded. In order to prevent anarchy the king had to rule firstly by travelling continually throughout his lands and secondly by appointing men that he could trust to govern under him. These royal officers were called 'mormaers'; the lands were then subdivided under the control of 'thanes'.

---

* *Palladius was the leader of a mission sent by Pope Celestine to the Scots.*

In spite of all the unrest, by the eleventh century life had blossomed, particularly for the nobility. The Celts were very artistic and in Scotland their culture had developed and flowered without the distraction and influence of Roman civilisation. People had reached a high standard of craftsmanship. They dressed in brightly coloured clothing worn with beautiful brooches, rings and pins. They had elaborate harnesses for their horses. Even their cooking and eating utensils were made with elegance and skill. They had a tradition of poetry and folk tales, which bards would recite as they travelled the country.

However, despite these elements of beauty in their lives, life was very hard for the ordinary people who lived around Arbuthnott. The bards and occasional travelling pedlars were some of the very few strangers that they would have seen, for each small community was very isolated. There were no roads and no towns. The largest settlements were made up of small groups of families. They had to be entirely self-sufficient and wrest a livelihood from the locality. They grew crops and raised sheep, goats, oxen and pigs, taking their livestock up to the higher ground in summer. They hunted wild game and fished in the river. Trades and crafts were handed down from father to son. When they or their livestock were ill they had to look for natural remedies, either from herbs or from curative waters, like the Bothenoth.

So life was precarious, the danger came from marauders, either Norsemen or Saxons raiding from the sea, or roaming bands of outlaws or highlanders coming down from the hills. The people needed protection and this they got from their thane; they were the thane's men, working for him and coming under his jurisdiction.

### The Coming of Feudalism

Scotland was gradually becoming a nation, but until the eleventh century, it still remained a Celtic civilisation. Then this quiet, insular way of life under its native ruling class and the haphazard structure of the Celtic Church was slowly destroyed by the relentless progress northwards of a new system of government which came to dominate both the people and the Church. This was the feudal system and came with the mighty castle-building Normans and their Roman Catholic clergy. It took over a century to complete but the process began after the Norman Conquest of England in 1066.

In England, William the Conqueror subdued the people by force and had no compunction in annihilating a rebellious population. In Scotland however the conquest was handled comparatively peacefully, though there was no choice for those concerned. The new lairds quite often married into the families of the Celtic thanes, and this is believed to be the case with the lairds of Arbuthnott. Evidence for this is that Duncan, a popular Christian name with earlier generations of the family, is a Celtic not a Norman or Anglo-Saxon name.

Under the feudal system all the land belonged to the king. He then granted or leased it to his followers in holdings known as baronies. The granting of land involved a ceremony where the subject knelt down and put his hands between those of the seated king in a gesture of submission. Thus the king's man became his vassal, swearing an oath of allegiance, and promising to supply men and arms in time of war. The vassal was given a written charter which detailed the extent of the property and the rights and privileges of the holder. It also specified the number of men and arms required for military service, which were to be supplied by the vassal in exchange for his holding. This fighting force was expected always to be in a state of readiness, because in times of war they would be immediately summoned to fight for the king. The number of men depended on the wealth of the property. Arbuthnott was almost certainly granted as a 'knight's fee'. This meant that the property was estimated to have enough wealth to provide the necessary number of men and horses needed to support a knight when he went to war.

In the case of the reorganisation of the Church under the feudal system, the bishoprics or dioceses were to be defined and established. The bishops, like the king, supervised their areas by travelling through them, always staying on church lands. These lands, which lay round the kirk and were used to maintain and feed the clergy, were granted by the king. Later, following his example, landholders granted portions of their lands in return for the prayers and goodwill of the Church.

## King Malcolm Canmore and Queen Margaret

This reorganisation, and that of the Church in particular, first began in Scotland in the reign of Malcolm Canmore and his wife, Queen Margaret. Malcolm Canmore came to the throne in 1057. Canmore meant 'Big-Head' or, more happily, 'Great Leader'. Malcolm was brought up at the English court from the age of nine, where he had been exiled following his father, King Duncan's murder at the hands of Macbeth. There he had learnt to admire the southern way of life. When he grew up he was restored to the throne with the help, among others, of Macduff, Earl of Fife. He married the English Princess Margaret as his second wife. She had fled north to Berwick with her brother Edgar Atheling, rightful claimant to the English throne, following the Norman Conquest. Both she and Malcolm had a determination that Scotland should leave her Celtic ways.

Margaret had been brought up partly in Hungary, at that time newly converted to Christianity, where she became a lady of strong and pious character. She was horrified at what she considered to be the lax habits of the Celtic Church and so, while acting with sympathy towards the Culdees, the Celtic semi-monastic group, she set about reforming the church and giving it a new Roman look. It was said "the Celtic Church brought love, the Roman Church the law" and it was this law that she set about establishing. She made the clergy become celibate and use the Roman calendar of feasts and saints days, and it was she who introduced a clear hierarchical structure to the Church. Such was her influence and example that she was later canonised and became known as

St Margaret of Scotland.

## *David I*

King Malcolm and Queen Margaret had eight children; three of their sons became Scottish kings. The youngest and greatest of these, David I, became king in 1124 and reigned for nearly 30 years. He was brought up in England and held an English barony. King David shared his mother's religious enthusiasm and continued to found religious houses and encourage a firm structure for the Church in Scotland as first promulgated by St Margaret.

He also carried on vigorously the process of imposing the feudal system on Scotland, granting his Norman and English friends baronies in return for their 'fealty' or vassalship. He created the first burghs, small towns where men were allowed to trade under his jurisdiction. They were established at strategic points, either a crossroads or at a port. This gave him revenue and for this he introduced currency for the first time to Scotland. He also set about making a parliament of barons and bishops. He set up sheriffs in areas known as counties, with a castle as their base. Sheriffs were also known as 'foresters', one of their duties being to maintain areas where the king could carry out the popular medieval sports of hunting and falconry. These royal hunts were splendid occasions in which the local thanes were invited to partake. One royal hunting ground included the Hill of Garvock and the northern slopes overlooking the Bervie Water.

King David's grandson, King William I (later known as William the Lion, because he introduced the Lion Rampant to the Scottish coinage and the Standard) inherited the throne in 1165 and immediately made a treaty with France. This was the beginning of the 'Auld Alliance', a centuries long friendship between France and Scotland with England as the common enemy; a move made necessary by the English kings' ambitions to bring the Scots under their feudal dominion.

Stonehaven

Dunnottar

Glenbervie

Fiddes

*Strathfinella Hill*

Fordoun

Kair

Pitarrow

Boghall

**ARBUTHNOTT**

Pitcarles

Kinneff

Allardice

*Banff*

Hallgreen

Inverbervie

Laurencekirk

*Hills of Garvock*

Gourdon

*KINCARDINESHIRE*

# Chapter 2

## The Founding of the Family

It was during the reign of William the Lion that the feudal redistribution of land reached the area now known as Angus and the Mearns. William built a castle at Montrose and from there he imposed his organisation on the surrounding area. He granted the lands of Arbuthnott to Osbert Oliphant. The Oliphant family were high in royal favour and Osbert had already been appointed Sheriff and Forester of the Mearns. Osbert's father, David Oliphant, was King David I's godson, and had once saved the King from capture after defeat in a battle near Winchester. He was an elderly adviser to King William when the Arbuthnott lands were settled on his son. In 1174 King William embarked on a disastrous war against the English and was taken as prisoner to France, where at Falaise he had to submit to the English King as his feudal overlord. So he must have granted the lands of Arbuthnott to Osbert Oliphant between 1170 and 1174, or around 1178 when he was again in the area and founded the Abbey at Arbroath.

Osbert Oliphant had 'taken the cross', a vow to fight in the Crusades from which he could only be released by special permission of the Pope. Therefore by 1190 he left for the Holy Land, despite being granted his own lands. King Richard the Lionheart of England was setting up a crusade at that time and Osbert probably went to join him. Arbuthnott was left under the management of his brother Walter. Walter, who had other concerns, soon leased the land to one Isaac of Benvie for six years, then later, on hearing of Osbert's death abroad he granted the estate to Hugh de Swinton. Some records say that Walter was Osbert's son or nephew rather than his brother, but had this been so it is more likely that he would have kept the lands of Arbuthnott for himself.

Hugh is the true founder of the family. He came up from the borders, a member of an ancient Anglo-Saxon family, which could trace its ancestry back nine generations to Edulf Edulfing, 1st Lord of Bamburgh in Northumberland (who died in 912 AD). He was related, possibly a grandson, to Cospatrick de Swinton, who fled from William the Conqueror, was given refuge by Malcolm Canmore and was later recorded as having received the Earldom of Dunbar or March.

There is a strong tradition that Hugh de Swinton became the new thane or laird of Arbuthnott because he married into the Oliphant family and in this way inherited the Arbuthnott lands. The Arbuthnott coat of arms certainly incorporates the Oliphant crescent. One theory put forward in a 1977 BBC Schools production was that the widow of the old Celtic thane married Osbert, and that their daughter married Hugh de Swinton. Principal Arbuthnott, the first historian of the Arbuthnott family, said that Osbert was related to Hugh:

> *Whom I find to have been related to the noble Sheriff of the Mearns of that time, called Osbert Olifard and, when this Osbert went with other Christian princes, to the war undertaken by Godfrey de Boulogne against the Saracens, the lands of Arbuthnott fell into the hands, first of Walter Olifard, and after him to Hugh Arbuthnott, who was descended from the most renowned house of Swinton, Earls of March at that time, as the self same documents record.*

## Hugh de Swinton, first Laird of Arbuthnott
## c.1190-c.1200

When Hugh de Swinton first came to Arbuthnott he found that the people still lived much as they had in late Celtic times, scattered in small communities which were joined by rough tracks and had little connection with the outside world. The land was rented from the laird, for whom every man was obliged to work a certain number of days, and to pay rent in kind, with milk, cheese, meat or grain. The seed was divided into three parts, one for the next sowing, one for food and one for rent, "*ane tae saw, ane tae gnaw and ane tae pay the laird witha*". The land was divided into 'ploughgates' of about 104 Scots acres, which was the area that could be worked by the eight oxen needed to pull the cumbersome ploughs. Men grouped together to rent the land and supply the team. They employed other men to help them. The oxen liked music so, if one man walked backwards in front of the team while whistling, they kept step and worked better. On the small and narrow patches a man working with one ox and a small plough could work an 'oxgate' of about 13 acres.

The land was divided up between the tenants and apportioned by drawing lots; the better land was cultivated, the rest was left for pasture. Most of the ploughing had to be done on the slopes because the flat and low lying ground was marshy. This meant that tillable land was at a high premium. Living conditions were primitive as there was no sanitation and houses were made of rough stones. Their roofs were made of turf with a hole through which the smoke had to escape. There was no glass, the wind was kept out by boarding over the windows and putting hides over doors.

When Hugh became "*dominus et thanus de Aberbothenoth*" (lord and thane of Arbuthnott) under the feudal system, he had complete authority over the tenants living on his lands. He held courts of justice where he had the power of life and death. As Principal Arbuthnott put it:

> *Within their own barony they had the power to hold courts and to apprehend certain offenders caught red-*

*banded, and to arrest criminals and outlaws and to put
some sorts of offenders to death.*

It was long held that the Criminal Mound, a small hill in a field between
Arbuthnott House and the kirk, was the scene of the old administration of justice. Another very important power that the laird held was over the mill-rights
within his lands. This meant that he alone could own a mill; his tenants were
bound to use it and had to pay a toll or fee for having their corn ground. Until
1839, when the eighth Viscount moved it to below the kirk, the mill occupied a
site at the south east corner of the garden about one hundred yards from
Arbuthnott House.

## The Kirkton Dispute

There were, however, some at Arbuthnott who were exempt from the rule of
the laird. When the lands of Arbuthnott were granted by William the Lion he
did not have the power to include the church lands, the few acres round the
kirk. These, along with jurisdiction over its tenants, belonged to the Church, in
this case the diocese of St. Andrews. Hugh and his son Duncan refused to
acknowledge this fact and came into dispute with the powerful Bishop of St
Andrews. In 1206 a Church Synod meeting at Perth made a judgement on the
case. In this pronouncement Duncan is styled as *"de Aberbothenoth"*, the first
man to use the name. There is no record of his defence, but the accounts of
thirteen witnesses for the Church are given and from them we have an authen-
tic description of life at Arbuthnott.

The first witness was John of Hastings, who was Sheriff and Forester of the
Mearns when Osbert *"possessed the lands in debate"*. In that position he
would have heard complaints from those who disputed the authority of the
laird. He asserted that there were many tenants on the church lands, and that
they came to him and showed him a *"Breive of our Sovereign Lord the King"*,
which stated that they were Bishop's men and so came under his jurisdiction
and not that of the civil authorities. The Kirkton tenants also had special rights
concerning the mill. (The Kirkton was the kirk village and the lands that went
with it).

The main witness was Isaac of Benvie, part of whose testimony is worth quot-
ing:

> *Isaac Beneain depones* [testifies] *that in the time of Bishop
> Hugh and Osbert Olifard, when the said Osbert took on the
> Jerusalem cross for an expedition to the Holy Land, he farmed
> the Kings revenue due out of the lands of Kirktown from the
> said Osbert as possessor thereof, and at that time the Kirktown
> had good bigging* [buildings] *on it, and there were upon the
> Kirktown eight tenants who were called goodmen, beside sub-
> tenants who had houses in the town and beasts feeding upon
> the pasturage. That Osbert's due out of the said town at that
> season was ten cheeses out of every reeking* [smoking i.e. inhab-

ited] *house within the Kirktown, made of the whole of their milk, fifteen days either before or after the feast of St John the Baptist and that for shearing his corns in harvest, he had out of every house three men one day by way of bondage. Depones that the foresaid Osbert informed him that the inhabitants of the Kirktown were bound to furnish their quota of provisions for the King's retinue, when going upon any expedition. Being interrogated about the mill, answered that the tenants in that town had a privilege of grinding their victual every Friday mul-ture [milling-fee] free, and that when the deponent insisted against them that they should be obliged to pay as others did who were Osbert's men, they shewed him a place where had been formerly a mill on their own lands which they had a power to rebuild, which when he understood to be truth, he agreed the matter with them, believing that it was in vain for him to contend with them, whom the Bishop always defended as his own men. That when the deponent inquired of Osbert what right he had upon their lands and possessions when any of the tenants were removed by death, Osbert replied that he had no right to sit tack [hold the lease] there, but all was in the power and disposition of the Bishop, as being his own property to give the land and houses to whom he pleased, and when one of the name of Gillandris, who was a cripple, was an inhabi-tant of that town, and more stiff than the rest, Osbert thinking that if he was removed the others would be more pliable, he offered the Bishop a horse worth five marks to remove him, which the Bishop understanding that he was a native of the place, would in no wise consent to.*

The other witnesses all supported Isaac's story, that Duncan had displaced the tenants and taken the land as his own and told of how the Bishop "*received entertainment from the inhabitants of that town as from his own men*". The testimonies reveal that thirteen thanes and at least six bishops had come and gone, so the lands had been given to the church by the King a long time before the lands were granted to Osbert Oliphant, possibly in the early days of King David or, judging from one testimony, as long as it would have taken for the mill building to have become a ruin.

The testimonies also show that the Kirkton tenants not only paid rent in cheeses but also had to help the laird with the harvest. Apart from their right to use the mill free of charge on a Friday they must have appeared to have much the same status as any other tenant at Arbuthnott. The high turnover of thanes would also have led to great confusion by the time Hugh took over the lands. His actions were, none the less, probably prompted by the fact that the disputed lands were among the richest and best in the area. So it is not surpris-ing that Hugh de Swinton and his son, Duncan, finding, as they did, a situation where the Church seemed unable to enforce the rights of its tenants, tried to incorporate the lands with their own. They might have managed it, but about that time the Bishop of St Andrews had his authority strengthened by a change in the status of the Church in Scotland.

Because the Scottish Church had no Archbishop of its own during the latter part of twelfth century, the Archbishop of York tried repeatedly to bring it under his jurisdiction. This move was strongly resisted by the Scots and finally in 1192, the Pope, having had a difference of opinion with the English monarchy, put the Church in Scotland directly under his rule, calling it his "*special daughter*". The Bishop of St Andrews, having an extremely large diocese which stretched from Berwick to Aberdeen, was therefore in a very powerful situation answerable only to the Pope. However communications were very slow and with such a large diocese to administer, there was little the Bishop could do quickly to reassert his authority over the Kirkton at Arbuthnott. He had to wait until the next Synod was convened, the witnesses brought (one testimony having been taken from a man on his deathbed), and the necessary scribes and officials gathered, which in those times must have been a formidable task. The eight hundred year old account, taken down so meticulously by a church scribe, gives a record of how the Arbuthnotts first came to their lands, the circumstances of which would otherwise be unknown. It conjures up a remarkable picture of the times, and especially of the thrawn Gillanders (his name meant 'one-legged') whose stubborn stance made Osbert attempt to trade him for a horse.

What do we know of Hugh de Swinton, first Laird of Arbuthnott? The younger son of an ancient house, he arrived at Arbuthnott in about 1190, probably penniless and possibly marrying the daughter of his predecessor. The Perth Synod testimonies imply that he died well before 1206.

### Duncan de Aberbothenoth, second Laird
### c.1200-c.1240

We know, from sources other than the Perth Synod testimonies, that Hugh de Swinton had at least one other son besides Duncan, called Alwin. They are both mentioned as witnesses to charters from which we learn that lands at Kinneff and Fordoun had been granted to Arbroath Abbey, also that a serf or 'nativus' had been given with his family to the church at St Andrews.

Duncan inherited Arbuthnott 'cum nativi'; he owned the serfs and tried to extend his powers to those at the Kirkton. A serf belonged to his lord and could be lent or given away; this was the reason why Gillanders was so determined to establish that he belonged to the Bishop of St Andrews. There were two sorts of tenant at the Kirkton, the more senior being the parsons or 'scolacs' who were church officials and under them the natives or serfs.

It may seem strange that Duncan had to submit to a judgement made in an Ecclesiastical Court. The Bishop however did not only have his authority straight from the Pope but, thanks to King David's patronage, the Church was becoming more and more rich and powerful; in time more so than the Crown itself. This inevitably led to its slow corruption and by the time the church lands were finally granted to the Laird of Arbuthnott, three hundred years later, the Reformation was on its way. They were granted in 1544 to Robert, fourteenth Laird, by the notorious Cardinal Beaton, a principal protagonist in the Reformation of the sixteenth century.

Principal Arbuthnott said of Duncan:

> *This Duncan lived in the days of King William and of his son Alexander the second and was of great reputation among the Mearns men for his quick wit in handling matters, but we want* [lack] *all writings concerning his deeds through the injury of time.*

From one charter we know he was still alive in 1238, but probably died soon after, as there is evidence of building activity by 1242, which indicates a change of laird.

### Hugh, third Laird of Arbuthnott c.1240-c.1260

The first and second Lairds would have lived on the easily defendable site now occupied by Arbuthnott House. In their time it would have been a mainly wooden one-storey building with surrounding ramparts. If invasion was threatened from the sea, there was a good view down to the river and the people could either flee to the hills or shelter inside the defences and hold out against attack. The oldest stonework to be found at the house dates back to around 1242, by which time it is likely that Hugh, son of Duncan, was third Laird. Hugh employed stonemasons to start work on building him a home.

The Bishop of St Andrews at that time was David de Bernham, an energetic and powerful man. He had been Lord Chamberlain of Scotland under Alexander II, son of William the Lion. In 1242 he held a Synod Council in the presence of the King and set down a Constitution, which "*secured the clergy in their possession and rights*". He then undertook to complete, over several years, the formal consecration of 140 kirks in his diocese, including Angus and the Mearns. There can have been no official record of any previous consecration of these kirks. It was on the 3 August 1242 that he came to Arbuthnott. Preparations for this occasion would have engaged the energies of the whole community for a considerable time. Suitable food and accommodation had to be prepared for the Bishop and his retinue, and the kirk itself was repaired for the occasion. In this the Church was helped by Hugh, third Laird. Masonry work similar to that found at Arbuthnott House and dating from the same time is also to be found in the walls of the kirk. Harry Gordon Slade, writing his report, *Arbuthnott House*, states "*It is a safe presumption that the same masons worked on both buildings*".

The ceremony would have been a rich and colourful one with many clergy participating in the long and elaborate service. New vestments, books, ornaments and furnishings would have been provided to celebrate the consecration; it was the responsibility of the priest to provide these. The priest got the revenue to pay for them and all other expenses as 'teinds' or tithes from his parishioners who were obliged to pay one tenth of their income to the Church.

In August 1992 the seven hundred and fiftieth anniversary of Bishop David's progress was celebrated in those churches still surviving and used for worship in Angus and the Mearns, including the Kirk of St Ternan, Arbuthnott.

Principal Arbuthnott has little to say about Hugh:

> *Duncan* (second Laird) *had a son Hugh, of whom I can find nothing to write except his name. But he must have been a man of great activity because we read that by his son's time the family was flourishing, and had been enriched with many lands.*

### Hugh le Blond, fourth Laird c.1260-c.1300

> *For his son kept his father's name, Hugh, and was known as Hugh the Blond because of his long yellow hair which he wore loose [quhilk he weir fyd].*

The fact that Hugh, fourth Laird, was known as Hugh le Blond on account of his long blond hair has given him an aura of romance which in past times has made him the hero of legends. His is still the identity given to the stone effigy in the Arbuthnott family aisle at the kirk, though from the style of the shield and chainmail it could be that of his father. The tomb on which it lies is of a later period. An added factor may be that during his lifetime Scottish history entered into a tragic and unruly era, in fact it would be many centuries before times were as good again as they were under the immediate heirs of Malcolm Canmore.

William the Lion was succeeded by his son, Alexander II (1214-49) and in turn by his grandson, Alexander III (1249-86). During this time there was peace between England and Scotland and a time of comparative tranquillity. The Vikings withdrew from Scotland under friendly terms and with a royal marriage between Margaret, the daughter of Alexander III and Eric, King of Norway. Then tragedy struck. Alexander was killed by a fall from his horse. His children had all died and his heir was his little Norwegian granddaughter who was declared Queen. The little girl, known as the 'Maid of Norway', died in Orkney in September 1290 on her way to Scotland, when she was only eight years old. From then on an era of turmoil ensued. Not only was there no obvious heir to the throne, but Edward I of England was bent on acquiring Scotland as his own, in the same way as he had subdued Wales.

The only facts we know of Hugh le Blond's life concern his landholding in the Mearns, at Arbuthnott and at the Hill of Garvock. A small part of the barony on Garvock Hill is mentioned in a charter:

*Charter by Hugh, called the Blond, lord of Aberbuthenoth, to the Church and Monks of Arbroath, in pure and perpetual alms, of one oxgate of land in which is situated the Church of Garvock, with the patronage of said church, and with pasture for 100 sheep, four horses, 10 oxen, 20 cows, and one bull, with fuel and other easements.*

*Dated at Arbroath, 2nd August 1282.*

Hugh le Blond's relations with the Church were clearly more peaceable than those of his great-grandfather and ancestral namesake, Hugh de Swinton.

*Tradition has it that the worn effigy in the Arbuthnott Aisle is the dashing dragon-slayer Hugh le Blond, 4th Laird (fl.1282) though it is probably his more prosaic father, Hugh. The effigy has been placed onto a tomb which is thought to belong to James, 13th Laird who died in 1521 despite a pilgrimage to Amiens.*

The first of the two legends concerning Hugh le Blond has already been mentioned; it told of his having slain a dragon with a two-handed sword at the Den of Pitcarles. An ancient two-handed sword hangs on a wall at Arbuthnott House. In times past it was thought to have been the one used by the fourth Laird. It is, however, a sword of the type fashioned in the second half of the fifteenth century and so was made long after the days of Hugh le Blond. It was never used in battle, instead it was used ceremonially as a symbol of the laird's authority. It was carried in front of the laird when he entered his court to administer justice.

The other legend made Hugh le Blond the subject of a ballad first printed by Sir Walter Scott in *The Minstrelsy of the Scottish Border*. The words were said to have been written down from a recitation of an old woman at Arbuthnott. The story bears a marked similarity to that told of Queen Guinevere, a tale in the true chivalric tradition which tells of a Queen, falsely accused of adultery, appealing for a knight to champion her cause and challenge her accuser to a tournament. By winning the contest, the champion would prove her innocence through trial by combat. The Queen, having been condemned to death by burning for adultery, was tied to the stake and awaited the arrival of her saviour. At the last moment he appeared, defeated the false accuser and the Queen was released. In this version it is Hugh le Blond who takes up the challenge, wins the tournament and is rewarded with the lands of Arbuthnott

> *The Queen then said unto the King*
> *"Arbattle's near the sea;*
> *Give it to the northern knight*
> *That this day fought for me."*
>
> *Then said the King, "Come here, Sir Knight,*
> *And drink a glass of wine,*
> *And if Arbattle's not enough*
> *To it we'll Fordoun join."*

Hugh le Blond was, however, the fourth generation to hold the lands of Arbuthnott. We can hear from Principal Arbuthnott that life was in reality a great deal less romantic:

> *Hugh le Blond lived in the days of Alexander III, and of John*
> *Balliol, at which time there was no King, when William Wallace*
> *personally undertook to defend the land which Henry King of*
> *England invaded and mercilessly ruined, and laid waste every-*
> *thing in the realm.* [The Principal probably meant King Edward rather than King Henry.]

To understand the background to this conflict we have to go back 6 generations to King David I who had two granddaughters, Margaret and Isabel. John Balliol, the claimant to the throne of whom the Principal writes, was the grandson of Margaret while Robert Bruce, the competing claimant, was great-grandson of Isabel. In 1292, two years after the little Maid of Norway died, the all-powerful Edward I of England, aptly named 'Hammer of the Scots' upheld the claim to the throne of John Balliol against that of Robert Bruce. King Edward invaded Scotland in 1296. He conquered the country, holding court at various castles and making 2,000 nobles pay homage to him. In July 1296, he reached the Castle of Glenbervie and there is every reason to believe that it was there that Hugh le Blond would have had to swear fealty. If he had not, he would have lost his lands. He may not have been the first, and was certainly not the last, laird of Arbuthnott who had to measure the wisdom of bowing to the overpowering forces of the time or losing his position. He, like the rest, took the pragmatic view and remained on his lands.

That same year, after constant warfare, John Balliol was finally deposed and abdicated at Stracathro, near Brechin. For ten years Scotland had no King. It was left to William Wallace to carry on the fight against Edward I, whom he never acknowledged as his overlord. After years of guerilla war, Wallace was finally captured by Edward in 1305 and taken to London, where he was given the brutal traitor's death of hanging, drawing and quartering, which Edward himself devised. Parts of his body were displayed at Newcastle, Berwick, Stirling and Perth as a warning to others.

King Edward even appointed the vicar to Arbuthnott Kirk in 1299, one Henry of Graystok. This man may never have seen his church but he got the teinds from it and appointed a substitute. The practice of an absentee vicar taking the income from the parish and putting a deputy in his place was quite common.

# Chapter 3

## Of Kings and Kettles

Resistance had not died with the death of William Wallace; the next year in 1306 Robert Bruce was crowned King at Scone, claiming the throne through his descent from David I. To claim the throne, however, he had killed his nearest rival in a church and was excommunicated by the Pope. With this blight on his life and the presence of English soldiers in all the main castles of Scotland, Bruce became a fugitive in his own kingdom and for many years, even after the death of Edward I in 1307, suffered endless setbacks in his fight to regain the independence of Scotland. It is of this time that the story is told of how Bruce, while lying hidden in a cave, watched a spider trying repeatedly to climb up to the roof. When he saw it at last gain its objective he was inspired to continue his struggle. He ousted the English from everywhere except the castle at Stirling and, in 1314, he finally defeated the English army close by Stirling at the Battle of Bannockburn.

### Duncan, fifth Laird c.1300-1314

We do not know the year in which Hugh le Blond died, but he was succeeded by his son Duncan, whose exact date of death was recorded. Again let us turn to our original family chronicler, Principal Alexander Arbuthnott, for a description of the times.

> *Hugh le Blond was succeeded by Duncan, named after his grandfather [great-grandfather], who was always gentle and peaceable. I have nothing to write about him except that he died a fair death in Arbuthnott on St Luke's Day 13 December 1314. At that time the most valiant prince Robert Bruce, the first of that name, rang in Scotland. This man [Duncan] gave the lands of Fiddes as a dowry for his daughter.*

So Duncan, fifth Laird, died in the year of the Battle of Bannockburn.

### Duncan, sixth Laird 1314-c.1320 and Hugh, seventh Laird c.1320-c.1350

The early fourteenth century is not well recorded as far as the Lairds of Arbuthnott are concerned, the only certain date is that of the death of Duncan, fifth Laird. Little is known of Duncan, sixth Laird or his son, Hugh, seventh

Laird. We have to gauge the dates of their lives from the history given by Principal Arbuthnott.

In 1320, six years after Duncan, sixth Laird succeeded, Edward II of England asked the Pope to renew the excommunication of King Robert the Bruce. The Scots reacted strongly. The nobles, clergy and commons all gathered at Arbroath and drew up a declaration to send to the Pope. They declared their loyalty to Robert Bruce as their King and their belief in Scotland's right to independence. Edward I had achieved one thing by his brutal wars. He had united the Scottish nation. However in a short time events went from bad to worse in the country as a whole.

> *After this man followed another Duncan who enjoyed the same good name as his father. These two lived in the days of David Bruce when the country was miserably torn apart by the Balliol faction*

In 1328 the Treaty of Northampton had been signed whereby Edward II recognised the independence of Scotland and Robert Bruce as rightful King, which should have augured well for the Scots. But Robert Bruce died in 1329 when his son David was only five. This ushered in two centuries of misery and strife. After three brief years a rebellion broke out and Edward Balliol, son of John, was proclaimed King. David II was sent to exile in France. As he returned to govern in 1341, aged seventeen, he was shipwrecked at King David's Head by Inverbervie. On landing he made the town a Royal Burgh, with the right to trade abroad. By 1346, he was at war with England, where he was taken prisoner and spent many years more of his long reign in exile. He was eventually released for a ransom of 100,000 marks, a ruinous sum for the country, which was at the same time suffering from flooding and the first visitation of the Black Death in 1349-50.

It is possible that Hugh, seventh Laird died at the time of the outbreak of plague since we know that his successor, Philip, was already Laird when lands were given to the Church in 1355.

### Philip, eighth Laird c.1350-c.1400

After four Hughs and three Duncans the succession in the Arbuthnott family passed to the eighth Laird with a new name, Philip. We can only speculate on the reason for this unusual Arbuthnott name, perhaps his mother had a French connection. Though we do not know his mother's identity, we do know that of his two wives, the first two to be mentioned in the Arbuthnott family.

Philip, eighth Laird's first wife was a Keith. The Keith family had come to live at Dunnottar Castle by the end of the fourteenth century. The head of the family had the title of Great Marshal, later Earl Marshal, and had the hereditary appointment of keeper of the crown jewels. Dunnottar was an impregnable stronghold on the coast, only a short ride north of Arbuthnott. The Lairds of

Arbuthnott married a Keith daughter on six occasions. Philip was the first. Janet Keith was his first wife and died leaving him two young daughters.

In 1880 Sir William Fraser published a report on the manuscripts then in the Charter Chest at Arbuthnott House. Here is the extract from this report, the *Fraser Papers*, concerning the eighth Laird:

> *Philip having no male heirs by his first wife, Janet, who was a daughter of Sir William Keith, Great Marischal of Scotland, gave his two daughters honourably in marriage with large portions, without partitioning his estate. Philip then dreading the ancient house should be ruined through division of the heritage between his daughters, so grieved about the matter that, from that or other causes he fell into "ane heavie disease". Thinking himself dying, he summoned his father-in-law to ask his advice, and especially as to waiving the right of his daughters to a partition of the estate. To which Lord Marischall answered frankly, "as the natur of men is addicted in their avin particular, lytill regarding the weill of wtheris"* [it is in the nature of man to be concerned with his own affairs, with little regard to the good of others], *that he need not trouble himself with that matter, for a sufficient provision was made to his grandchildren by the laws, as the whole property would fall to them, and advised him to be careful to recover his own health and to leave his daughters alone. Philip of Arbuthnott took this advice deeply to heart, and being determined to preserve his family inheritance intact, after bidding a courteous farewell to his father-in-law, he began to take 'good courage' and strove against his weakness. The result was that his sickness passed off, and he gradually regained his former health. To promote his convalescence, however, as soon as he was able to travel, he went, carried in a litter, to Edinburgh there to obtain the benefit of medical advice. As his strength returned he began to think of marrying again, and visiting frequently at the Castle of Dalkeith held by Sir William Douglas, he found that "this lord had certane dochteris, virginis and meit for mariage". "Lyking their bewtie and conditionis" he* [Philip] *proposed to their father for one of them. Being accepted, the marriage was completed, as the family historian says, with magnificent preparations. The result gratified Sir Philip of Arbuthnott's wishes, as his wife bore him a son Hugh, who inherited the estates, and many other children.*

It sounds as if Philip had what we would now call a nervous breakdown brought on by his worries concerning the future of the Arbuthnott lands. If he had had no male heir his lands would have been divided between his daughters and the family name would have been lost. Luckily his second marriage to Margaret Douglas was fruitful and resulted in at least two children, the eldest of whom, Hugh, was the heir Philip had so desired. At the time of this second marriage Philip had a charter drawn up. It was for the lands of Arbuthnott in favour of his wife or himself, whoever lived longer, and the male heirs of that marriage. Witnessed by a relative of his wife, Archibald Douglas, Lord of Galloway and Bothwell, it was dated 25 October 1372.

While he was still a young man Philip became a benefactor to the church of the Carmelite Friars of Aberdeen.

> *Charter by Philip of Abirbothnot of that ilk, conveying to the Carmelite Friars of Aberdeen, an annual rent of thirteen shillings and four pence sterling, yearly, payable from his whole land of Abirbuthnot, towards the repair of the Church of said Friars.*

> *Dated at Aberdeen 25 April 1355.*

This grant was confirmed by David II, King of Scots on 13 August 1365.

Life for the general population was no easier than it had been in Philip's father's day. In 1361 there was a second outbreak of the Black Death. It spread from the south and may have been the basis of the old idea that houses should never be built facing south as it was from that direction that the wind brought the plague. On this occasion the pestilence reduced the population by a third, and although it spread far more rapidly in the towns, it is unlikely that Arbuthnott escaped the infection. The smaller population increased the value of labour and as a result serfdom began to die out.

Philip died in about 1400. After his death his widow Margaret Douglas had a fractionement (portion of the rent) of all the lands of Arbuthnott for her lifetime. Margaret gave them to her son in exchange for a yearly sum of money. Since he had inherited the main body of Arbuthnott lands this maintained them effectively in single ownership. The widow's provision made for Margaret shows one of the responsibilities of a laird. It became part of Scots law that a landowner's widow had the right to a 'terce', the revenue from a third of her husband's lands for her lifetime unless other provision was made. Another responsibility for the laird was the provision of a dowry for his daughters if they were to marry well, as Duncan, fifth Laird had provided Fiddes for his daughter.

Philip is the first Laird for whom we have enough evidence, albeit largely hearsay, to form some impression of his personality. He seems to have been a careful, fair man with more than a usual sense of dynastic responsibility.

### The Stuart Dynasty

When David II, son of Robert Bruce died in 1371 he had no heir, so the crown passed to his nephew Robert, the son of his elder sister Margery. She had married Walter, holder of the hereditary office of Steward, hence the name Stewart or Stuart. This was the start of the Stuart Dynasty, which brought such trauma to the Scots for the next four hundred years. Of the first twelve Stuart monarchs (there were fifteen altogether), two were murdered, two executed, two died in battle, two others died prematurely (one of a riding accident), two were forced to abdicate and only three died of natural causes. Of the nine Stuart monarchs who ruled before the uniting of the crowns of England and Scotland, seven inherited as children owing to the early, usually violent, death of their parent. This led to long periods when the country was in the hands of regents, who were mostly self interested men with an eye to power and frequently the crown itself.

The first of the line was Robert II who found that, because he did not come from an ancient line of kings, the nobles failed to accept him. His reign was marked with rebellion and constant border raids. His son Robert III, who had been crippled by a kick from a horse five years before he came to the throne, proved unable to ride and lead his army and gradually his ambitious brother, the Duke of Albany, managed to take over. By 1402, the Duke of Rothesay, the King's elder son and the rightful heir to the throne, had disappeared, presumably murdered by his uncle Albany who then took over as Regent.

The next heir was twelve-year-old James who, in 1406, was sent to France by his father for his safety but was captured at sea by pirates (probably agents of Albany) and taken to England. The shock of the news of his capture killed the deposed King Robert. The young King James I spent the next eighteen years as a hostage at the English Court, while Albany ruled as Regent, making little effort to pay the ransom demanded for the King. Meantime the nobles strove to carve out kingdoms for themselves. Particularly successful in the lowlands was the Douglas family who built a power base in the south west with a large private army, hardened in the border wars. In the highlands the Chief of the MacDonalds was called 'Lord of the Isles'. He never recognised the Scottish King as his overlord, had a treaty with England and fought and lost a war to gain lands throughout Northern Scotland.

As a culmination to his long rule, in 1420 Regent Albany took all the customs money raised in Edinburgh for himself; this was the last act of a ruthless and selfish man. He died and was succeeded by his weak son Regent Murdoch. This was the man to whom Hugh, ninth Laird of Arbuthnott, in a famous incident, appealed over the arrogant behaviour of Sheriff Melville.

### Hugh, ninth Laird c.1400-1446

*Evin for Hew having all yingis going well wt him, put he haill houf in no small danger.*

*Even though Hugh had everything going well for him, he put his whole house in great danger.*

So said the Principal when he came to write of the ninth Laird of Arbuthnott. It was during this chaotic time in Scotland's history that Hugh, Philip's heir, who succeeded about 1400, became involved in the least happy episode in the history of the family, which took place near Garvock Hill at a spot since called the Sheriff's Kettle. Harry Gordon Slade tells the story succinctly, and it is as well to have his account rather than fall into the trap of which Principal Arbuthnott gave warning "*since I am descended from the same house I will leave it to others to recount as it may appear a greater place has been given to affection than to truth itself*".

> *On the whole the family history is free from those blood-drenched and melodramatic horrors usually only to be found in the pages of Scotch family histories and Gothick novels, and it was possibly the fact that his mother was a Douglas which accounts for the gruesome lapse on the part of Hugh Arbuthnott, ninth Laird. In 1420 John Melville of Glenbervie was Sheriff of the Mearns and, according to tradition, had incensed his neighbours by his tyranny. Probably his fault was that he had interfered too much in the exercise of their own particular tyrannies. On representations being made to the Regent, Murdoch Duke of Albany, that worthy commented "Sorrow gin that that Sheriff were sodden and suppit in broo'."* ["Would that that Sheriff be drowned and supped in broth"]. *With this somewhat dubious authority five lairds, Arbuthnott amongst them, invited the Sheriff to a hunting party in the Forest of Garvock. Once there he was knocked on the head, and his body thrown into a convenient cauldron. Having simmered this grisly mess for a while each of the friends downed a spoonful of the resulting soup. As Arbuthnott was, if not the prime mover in this outrage, Glenbervie's nearest neighbour, it was expected that he would be the first to feel the wrath of the Melvilles. The house was substantial but not strong enough to "debait the Invasion of Enemyes"; measures were quickly taken to strengthen it and the deed which had threatened Hugh with ruin gave him instead a greatly improved house and considerably enhanced the standing of the family; the latter apparently, according to Principal Arbuthnott, being a result of the former.*

Whatever the provocation, Principal Arbuthnott had a stern view of the Sheriff's misdemeanours:

> *At that time John Melville, a strong and forceful man, was Laird of Glenbervie, who, puffed up with riches and numerous dependents, chiefly because he had a great number of Highlandmen at his command, became very proud and plundered all the baronies around him, so that he daily did them great injury.*

Hugh was frightened after the murder into building a strongly fortified two storey castle. He never finished it perhaps because he had a way out of his predicament by claiming kinship to the Clan Macduff. Among the notes in the

*Fraser Papers* the advantage of this is explained:

> *According to tradition, any one who killed a man, if he were*
> *within nine degrees of kindred to Macduff who restored*
> *Malcolm III* [Malcolm Canmore] *to the Scottish throne, had this*
> *privilege* [*] *- he was entitled to betake himself to Macduffs Cross*
> *near Newburgh in Fife and there claim that on payment of a*
> *certain penalty he should be free from all other punishment.*

The price of the penalty was reputed to be the gift of nine cows and one heifer and on 13 September 1421 a letter of remission was granted to *"Hugh Arbuthnott of that Ilk, anent the slaughter of Johne Malavill of Glanbervy"*, also included in the pardon were all those who had assisted in the crime and helped Hugh to build his strong castle. The conspirators had a chapel built at Drumlithie where daily prayers were offered for the soul of Sheriff Melville, *"for men at that time were given to such superstition"* remarks Principal Arbuthnott.

Hugh's father, Philip, had married Janet Keith as his first wife and Hugh himself married her kinswoman, Margaret Keith. They had at least two children, including the heir, Robert. Margaret died on 28 November 1419 and so was spared the anguish of seeing her husband become a murderer. Perhaps grief at her death contributed to the reckless mood which prompted Hugh's actions. He lived on as a widower until 1446 by which time he was quite an old man.

---

[*] Privileges of consanguinity to the Clan Macduff:
- to seat the King in the Coronation Chair;
- to lead the van (front) of the Army;
- to compound by a fine in cases of homicide.

*Douglas, Peerage of Scotland (1764)*

# Chapter 4

## A Scottish Renaissance

*At the return of King James the miserable state of the Kingdom
by his wisdom was redressed to a prosperous and peaceable
state.*

So wrote Principal Arbuthnott, but the peace was not to last. While being held
hostage in England, James I had married the Lady Joan Beaufort, granddaughter
of John of Gaunt and cousin of the English King. It was reputedly a love-match.
In 1424 he returned to Scotland to reclaim his throne. He subdued the power
of the nobles but in so doing made enemies and was murdered in 1437. His
murder took place in front of his wife. The revenge she meted out to his mur-
derers by having them slowly put to death by torture puts Hugh, ninth Laird's
misdeeds into perspective.

Scotland was again under a regent, James II being only six years old. He grew
up to be an able and innovative man. He had to struggle constantly to gain
ascendancy over his nobles and their powerful families, still notably the
Douglas family, into which Philip Arbuthnott, eighth Laird, had married. As a
child James II witnessed the slaying of Earl Douglas at a dinner. He had learnt
to subdue his other nobles with equal vigour, often by taking their castles by
force. For this he had at his disposal a weapon too costly for anyone but a
monarch to possess. The age of gunpowder had arrived and with it the first use
of cannon, and Mons Meg survives at Edinburgh Castle as an example of the
size and unwieldiness of these early guns. They were crude, very heavy and
also extremely dangerous. The main expense they incurred was not only in
terms of the skilled operators, usually French, who manned them, but also the
men and horses needed to drag them across country. James II was naturally fas-
cinated and thrilled with this weapon, but at the siege of Roxburgh in 1460 he
stood too close to a cannon and was killed when it exploded. James III became
King aged ten. In this way the century progressed with much the same pattern
repeating itself, short periods of brilliant rule by a young monarch, sudden
death and another regency, giving the nobles, once again, the chance to regain
power.

James III, though, was not popular because he was introspective, intellectual
and chose the wrong friends. He did not even ride well and good horseman-
ship was still a vital attribute for a king; just how vital was to be proved by the
manner of his death. His brothers possessed those qualities that he lacked and

so they became a threat to his position. He therefore had them put in prison where one died; the other, another Duke of Albany, made a daring escape from Edinburgh Castle and went to England where he gathered an army, and marched north to fight against his brother. The King survived this invasion, though Albany became Regent for a while. However in 1488 after the Battle of Sauchieburn, where he again fought against his rebellious nobles, he was murdered by a man who, disguised as a priest, pretended to come to minister to him after he had had a bad fall from his horse. His fifteen-year-old son became King James IV.

From the outset the young James IV was well-loved, talented and able to control his nobles. There was a new flowering and confidence in his reign. Although life was still hazardous and travel impossible without an armed escort, Scotland was none the less beginning to establish her reputation for learning. The first Scottish university was founded at St Andrews in 1411, to be followed by Glasgow in 1451 and then King's College, Aberdeen in 1495. It was during the reign of James IV that a law was passed making it obligatory for landowners to educate their heirs. They were to learn Latin and, after they had reached the required standard, they were to study law and the arts for three further years. They would then be in the position to become judges and sheriffs. Failure to comply meant a fine of twenty pounds This was a new idea to many lairds, used as they were to the idea that prowess in warfare was far more important than scholarship. Thus it came about that the young sons of wealthier families started to travel to these Scottish cities, and even as far as France, for their education. Having reached these places they often stayed on and became established in trade and business, becoming burghers or city merchants.

The term 'burgher' needs explanation. We have seen that the feudal system was based on two strengths. There were the 'Lords Spiritual', the bishops, who derived their power from the authority of the Pope and the 'Lords Temporal', who held undisputed power within their lands through the king, to whom they owed services in exchange, particularly providing armed men for warfare and attending the court, council and parliament. This organisation may have been a good method of keeping law and order within the realm and defending it when invasion was threatened but it did not supply the king with an income. So when David I introduced the idea of founding burghs, back in the twelfth century, his main purpose was to raise revenue.

The burghs that King David I created were specific settlements, located either at ports or on trading routes. Here, in exchange for a levy, burghers or merchants were granted certain rights, the most important being the right to trade and, in the particular case of a royal burgh, the right to trade abroad. The inhabitants needed to defend themselves, and so were allowed to surround themselves with a protective wall. Within their boundary they could carry arms, have a limited power of self-government, and could organise their methods of trading. Towns grew up in which the power lay with the merchants and craftsmen who formed themselves into guilds. These towns became international communities, to which traders came from England, France, Germany, the

Netherlands and Scandinavia. Scotsmen thought nothing of travelling to these countries to trade, the strongest links always being with France. Another type of burgh, 'burghs of barony' traded locally, with the revenues going to the landowner.

Despite the growing prosperity of the burghs and the beginning of an established higher education system, in the main people lived in constant fear and unrest. The laird at Arbuthnott had to be permanently prepared for war. One of the duties of a feudal vassal was to keep his contingent of armed men constantly ready to take up arms. Ever since the establishment of the feudal system there had been regular training, but in 1457 Parliament made it obligatory to hold these training sessions or 'wapinshaws' at least four times a year. Archery butts were required to be built by statute and on certain Sundays the able-bodied men met for target practice. There was a fine of twopence for non-attendance which was spent on drink for those present. At Arbuthnott practices took place near the kirk.

Warfare was not the only preoccupation. Other activities took place beside the kirk on Sundays and other feast days, because church-going was the one occasion when people could leave their isolated communities and gather together. Pedlars traded at the kirk porch, and because it was the only sheltered meeting place, the kirk was used for gatherings, festivities and celebrations, to the extent that rules had to be made against wrestling and unruly behaviour within the kirk precincts. Before the Reformation, St Ternan's Day would have been one of the religious holidays; after the Reformation there were no more feast days and Sundays became a great deal more sedate.

Everything James IV did was approved by the majority; even his many mistresses and numerous illegitimate children were condoned, because in pre-Reformation Scotland standards of morality were very lax. The Church in Scotland as a whole had deteriorated badly since the days of the devout and efficient David de Bernham, Bishop of St Andrews. The clergy were corrupt, the parish priest was often a deputy who was paid a pittance while the revenue of the tithe or teind was appropriated either by an absentee rector or some religious institution. Little of the money went to the upkeep of church buildings which fell into disrepair through neglect. Appointments to the higher and more lucrative offices were given as livings to unsuitable protegés; young men of royal blood and the nobility were given bishoprics and priories so that they received the revenue but were far from suitable to carry out their duties. James IV had his illegitimate son appointed Archbishop of St Andrews while still a small child, and by the next century, corruption in church appointments had reached such an extreme that James V was able to make various of his illegitimate sons the Abbots of St Andrews, Holyrood, Melrose, Kelso, and Coldingham. The Church had become many times richer than the Crown and this was the way the King could redress the balance. After all he had eleven illegitimate children to support, while Cardinal Beaton, Archbishop of St Andrews, had only eight.

### Robert, tenth Laird 1446-1450

Hugh, ninth Laird was the fifth and last of that name, while his son was the first of ten lairds to be called Robert. Robert, tenth Laird married Giles Ogilvy, daughter of Sir Walter Ogilvy of Lintrathen, High Treasurer of Scotland,*"with whom he lived happily for a long time"*.

Principal Arbuthnott goes on to tell us that the old Laird Hugh, veteran of the incident of the Sheriff's Kettle, lived on to a great old age, kindly cared for by his son and daughter-in-law. His account is the only information we have about the tenth Laird.

> *he acted as the young laird, helping his father, who, in his old age, was unable to manage his affairs. Nor did he live long after his father, for five years after his father's death, in the year of God 1450, he departed this mortal life.* [The actual dates sug-gest four years.]

Robert, tenth Laird died on 21 February 1450 while King James II was still only nineteen, and his wife died on 4 May 1468. They had six sons and one daugh-ter. The heir was their first son, David and it is from their second son Hugh, that the Aberdeenshire branch of the family, the 'one t' Arbuthnots, are thought to be descended.

### David, eleventh Laird 1450-1470

Their eldest son David was Laird for twenty years until 1470. He married Elizabeth Durham and they had four daughters and two sons, the heir Robert, and Hugh who went to France, became a physician and settled there. Of this second son Hugh, Principal Arbuthnott writes that he:

> *being allured with the pleasantness and civility of that country, married and settled there with great honour. He left issue - but the names are changed as the fashion is there. And so the sur-name either lurks unknown or it is perished.*

David, eleventh Laird, died on 8 October 1470 and his wife Elizabeth lived on until 10 April 1488, like her mother-in-law surviving her husband for eighteen years. She died in the same year as King James III.

### Robert, twelfth Laird 1470-1506

No progress was made to complete the castle built by Hugh, ninth Laird until the time of his great-grandson, the great Laird Robert, who was described in his obituary as *"a man of great discernment, marked out by God"*. There is little wonder at the delay, the two intervening generations lived in frightening and difficult times. Added to which the trauma of the episode of the Sheriff's Kettle must have had a paralysing effect on the family, one which took a long time to wear off and that cast a shadow over two generations

Fifty years after the dark and dreadful deed of the murder of Sheriff Melville, the Arbuthnott family was in need of a laird of strength and moral vision. This they got with Robert, twelfth Laird, who, in 1470, inherited the same problems as his father and grandfather, the unfinished castle and the warlike and unsettled times. Principal Arbuthnott obviously held him in high regard, he was speaking of his grandfather when he wrote:

> *I now return to Robert, the eldest son, he was without question a man of outstanding ability, and held in great esteem among the people of the Mearns; by his foresight, his profuse generosity, his devotion to religion, his well-known hospitality, the number of dependents which he supported, in a word, by the many notable deeds which he accomplished, he left a family already full of honours even more honoured and renowned. To his natural ability was added a passing acquaintance with letters, and he enhanced these qualities by his wide experience; it is hardly surprising therefore that he should have developed into the complete and polished man he was. He it was who first apportioned the various offices and duties among his servants, and laid down for the Arbuthnotts a formal policy by which the family interest should be directed in a worthy fashion; a policy the traces of which still remain.*

Robert, twelfth Laird married twice, his first wife was Margaret Wishart, daughter of a neighbouring landowner, James Wishart of Pitarrow. She died leaving him a son, Hugh. Since Robert himself had *"a passing acquaintance with letters"*, he may have wanted his young son to have a better chance to learn and soon it was to become mandatory for the heirs of landowners to receive an education. Hugh was sent as a scholar to the college in Brechin which was run by two chaplains and where the boys were taught music, singing and Latin. The boys sang High Mass in the cathedral, as well as at other services. Their hair was cut in a tonsure and they wore black gowns with a fur-lined collar when they were within the cathedral precincts and when they went outside the city their dress was a dark blue ankle length tunic. Conditions may well have been very austere. Hugh was about fourteen when he died there on 2 March 1484.

Robert married Marion Scrymgeour as his second wife in 1475. They had five sons and seven daughters. Their eldest son, Ambrose, died on 22 July 1491. James, the second son, then became heir and the youngest, later known as 'Andrew in Pitcarles', was the father of Principal Arbuthnott. Even the pious Robert followed the trend of the day by having a 'natural' son, Patrick, an eminent man who became physician to James V after going to France for his education and training. In 1531 he received his letters of legitimation and died in 1540, having been Rector of Menmuir and Canon of Dunkeld.

Robert, twelfth Laird, received at least two letters from his sovereign demanding military assistance. One was from James III, dated 3 January 1483, at the time when his brother the Duke of Albany was leading an English army against him. The second letter was dated 22 September 1490 and was from James IV, writing from Stirling and telling him to *"fortify and secure his castle for the King's service"*.

The second letter no doubt spurred on efforts to finish the castle. In the family, Laird Robert is remembered more than anything for his building activities. The small castle built at Arbuthnott by Hugh, ninth Laird was more than doubled in size with two new blocks and a linking gatehouse. It must have been an impressive structure. For an account of Robert's activities, we can again turn to Principal Arbuthnott:

> *The castle, from the days of his great grand-father, Hugh, who had laid the foundations and built it up to the second floor, was lying incomplete and with no further extensions. Robert completed the work at great expense and added a roof; he decorated the top of the walls with eaves and projections as is usual in castles. At great pains he added a new building from the ground up, which is now called the Twin. Near the castle he also built another house in vaulted style and roofed it with thin stone slabs; the top part of this house, he appointed as a kitchen. He surrounded the front of the castle with a very high wall furnished with battlements; he built a splendid gate in vaulted style, and above it a house which is now called the front tower; this tower was afterwards extended and stoneproofed by his grandson who is now head of the family.*

Robert's interest was not confined to secular buildings. The kirk at Arbuthnott has not changed in its outside appearance since his day. The side chapel that he built is known as the Arbuthnott Aisle and is still used by the family as a burial place; the ashes of the fifteenth Viscount and thirty-second Laird and his wife are buried there.

> *First he completed the western part of Arbuthnott chapel in a more lavish style than had previously been employed; he built over it too a round tower designed as a belfry, and furnished it with two bells. Later at the eastern corner of the chapel, he built a side-chapel of cornered stone, with jutting projections and battlements above, striking both for the skill and materials employed. It is now called the Aisle of Arbuthnott. In the lower part of this building he raised a very high vault and provided it with an expensive altar and all the trappings which go with divine worship. The upper part of the building above the vault he appointed as a chamber for whoever should be sacristan. The lowest part of the crypt of this side-chapel he intended as a common burial place for the Arbuthnotts.*

*And lest it should seem that so splendid a building was con-
structed in vain, or should suffer loss through the negligence of
its keepers, he assigned to his successor an annual sum, in per-
petuity, of somewhat more than £10 Scots for its upkeep. And
that this work of his might be rendered more pleasing and
acceptable to God, he carefully saw to it that no part of the cost
of constructing so magnificent a building should fall on his tenants and least of all the poor, nor even as is sometimes the custom, that their beasts should be used for collecting the stones,
lime and the rest of the material necessary for the construction,
but only his own.*

**Robert, 12th Laird's Arbuthnott Aisle built around 1482**

As this account of Robert, twelfth Laird's achievements was written only sixty
years after his death, Principal Arbuthnott could describe in fascinating detail
the building work which his grandfather commissioned, giving us his picture of
a man of vision, a kindly and caring laird. There is no doubt that Robert had a

deep faith, which was shared by his second wife Marion Scrymgeour, and with her support he found the strength and inspiration to set about the building work.

As we have heard, piety was not in vogue at that time. The Church had become corrupt and ripe for reformation. At Arbuthnott, however things were altogether different. This was thanks to Robert, twelfth Laird, who went against the trend and made many contributions to the cause of his faith. He transformed the kirk at Arbuthnott in an age when most church buildings were falling into disrepair owing to the neglect and greed of the clergy. But this was by no means all that he did. The piety of the twelfth Laird is demonstrated by a series of surviving documents. Robert and his wife Marion gave money to the Order of Observantines, a branch of the Franciscan Order. One, to be found in the inventory of Arbuthnott writs, reads:

> *Indulgence by Brother John Litster of the minor brethren of the Observantines in Scotland, and Brother Emir de Hamel of the same order in those parts beyond the mountains, to Robert Arbuthnott of that Ilk and Marion Scrymgeour his lady for contributing to the Expedition to the Holy Land against the Turks, with the formal absolution granted thereupon.*

> *Arbuthnot, 30 April 1482.*

In 1487 they were received into the Fraternity of the Order. In 1491, the year their eldest son died, they were granted the great honour of a licence, by Pope Innocent VIII, to have their own portable altar, the right *"to carry ane altar and sua messis wher they pleas, in ony place convenient"*. They were then made a serving brother and sister of the Fraternity of St John of Jerusalem by Sir William Knollys, Preceptor of the Order at Torphichen.

During the time that elapsed between the events of Robert's life and Principal Arbuthnott's written account, the great upheaval of the Reformation had taken place. Because of this and the religious strictures of his time, even Principal Arbuthnott had to keep very quiet about the most significant contribution of all. Robert, twelfth Laird commissioned three illuminated manuscripts which are today the only surviving pre-Reformation documents of their kind.

Arbuthnott had at that time the unfashionable asset of a scholarly and devout parish priest. James Sibbald was a member of the family of the Sibbalds of Kair, the estate which marched with Arbuthnott to the west. Traditionally it has been said that it was in the priest's room, on the upper floor of the Arbuthnott Aisle that James Sibbald transcribed and illuminated three holy books, a missal, a prayer book and a psalter which Robert had commissioned. It is more likely that he performed this task nearby while the building work was being undertaken. Sibbald transcribed his beautifully illuminated manuscripts between 1482 and 1491. The psalter and prayer book were completed, the first in 1482 and the second in 1483 and were for the laird's personal use. There is an obituary of the Arbuthnott family between 1314 and 1551 at the back of the prayer book. It is in this that we can find details of the deaths of family members, including that of Duncan, fifth Laird and Robert's young sons Hugh and Ambrose. In the psalter there is a note written beside the date of the Battle of Flodden which was fought in 1513.

The Arbuthnott Missal is the only Scottish version in existence, in terms of saints honoured and the form of service laid out, the remainder having all been destroyed at the Reformation. Other surviving missals were all written either in the Sarum (English) tradition or in the Irish tradition. It contains Scottish saints, notably of course, St. Ternan, in its calendar of saints days. It was completed in 1491 and was dedicated to the Altar of St. Ternan and given to the kirk in celebration of the completion of Robert's building additions.

Robert meant the manuscripts to remain at Arbuthnott. At the end of the psalter he wrote: *"Let this book remain here till an ant drink dry the rivers and the seas, and a tortoise walk round the entire world"*. Sadly this was not to be. They remained in the possession of the Arbuthnott family until 10 December 1897 when they were sold at Sotheby's after the death of the tenth Viscount, when the family fortunes were reaching their lowest ebb. They were bought by the Coats family who donated them to the Paisley Library and Museum where they can now be seen.

Robert, twelfth Laird died in 1506, just surviving into the century which was to see fundamental changes in the established Church. It was as well he did not live to see his beloved Catholicism rooted out and replaced by the new religion. Within seventy years of his death, however, his own grandson, Principal Arbuthnott was to play a leading role in the establishment of the new Protestant faith.

Among the obituary notices at the back of his prayer book there is written, *"the death of Robert Arbuthnot of that ilk, a man of great discernment, marked out by God, founder of the Missal. Who died on the third day of the month of November 1506."* Robert, twelfth Laird stands out as the most notable of all the Lairds of Arbuthnott. While the castle he finished was largely pulled down and replaced with the present house, his religious legacies have survived intact to this day. This remarkable fact begs the question, how did his holy books survive the Reformation when most were destroyed? And why should the Kirk of St Ternan, Arbuthnott still look exactly as it did when he finished building his additions 500 years ago? Perhaps he was indeed *"marked out by God"*.

### James, thirteenth Laird 1506-1521

For an account of James, heir to the twelfth Laird, we can go to the second family history written by another Arbuthnott clergyman, the Reverend Alexander Arbuthnot, Episcopal minister at Arbuthnott from 1667-89. It begins:

*James who succeeded Robert the second, was the son of Marion*
*Scrimger, and married Jean Stewart Athol's daughter; by whom*
*he had two sons and one daughter. The eldest son was Robert*
*the third, the second called David Parson of Menmuir was killed*
*at Pinkie. His daughters name was Isobel was married first to*
*Ochtelony of Kelly and afterwards to Maule of Panmure. This*
*James got the holding ward changed to blanch. He was*
*removed by immature death in the flower of his age, in the year*
*1521, and to him succeeded Robert the third of that name, so*
*called after his grandfather.*

The significance of James getting the "*holding ward changed to blanch*" was that he converted his obligation as a feudal laird from giving military service to a monetary payment or feu. His tenure of the lands changed from a ward-holding to a 'feu-ferme'. Andrew, Bishop of Caithness issued his acquittance. James Wishart of Pitarrow is named as the man who delivered the payment of £100 which James had to pay. This change of the landowner from the old feudal status of 'vassal' to a 'feuer' gradually spread throughout Scotland. Feu-duty is only being phased out now, in the latter half of the twentieth century.

James, thirteenth Laird married Jean Stewart, daughter of the Earl of Atholl and a great-granddaughter of James I's queen, Joan Beaufort. After the death of her husband the twelfth Laird, James' mother Marion Scrimgeour is thought to have lived on the site of the present Banff farmhouse; she died in 1518. By 1520 James himself was a sick man. It was then that he was granted a licence under the Privy Seal in the name of James V, to go on a pilgrimage to France, to visit the shrine of St John of Amiens to seek a cure. Such were the binding obligations of a feudal baron that he required the permission of his overlord before travelling abroad. The licence was dated November 1520, but by the following March the pilgrimage had proved ineffectual and he had died.

# Chapter 5

## The Reformation

King James IV continued his successful reign, ever growing in popularity. For many years, while Henry VII, a pragmatic and peaceable man, reigned in England, there was peace between the two countries. In 1509 he was succeeded by his son, the impetuous and warlike Henry VIII. Even though James was married to Henry's sister, Margaret Tudor, a personal animosity grew up between the two kings, to the extent that when, in 1513, Henry invaded France and the French Queen appealed to James' chivalrous nature by sending him her ring, the Scottish king responded by calling up an army to support the French against the English. Such was their love and admiration for him that the flower of Scotland's nobility and all their best fighting men followed him to the Battle of Flodden, where they died beside him, leaving Scotland destitute and with an infant King. The whole of Scotland went into a state of shock after Flodden. The extent of the slaughter put nearly every noble household into mourning. A marginal note by September in the Calendar of the Arbuthnott Psalter reads:

> *Obiit Jacobus quartus rex Scotorum apud bellum de Floudane*
> *9 September anno domini 1513. Orate pro eo.*

> *James IV Kings of Scots died at the Battle of Flodden*
> *9 September 1513. Pray for him.*

An English invasion was expected but Flodden had taken such a toll of both sides that the English had no strength to pursue their victory. In the vacuum that was left James V became a pawn in the rivalry that grew up between powerful factions and he had a troubled childhood. He looked to France for a wife. His first bride died young and he then married Mary of Guise. England under Henry VIII remained hostile, with the added factor that Henry had now broken with the Catholic Church over his divorce from his first wife, Catherine of Aragon, and was keen to establish Protestantism throughout Britain. James with his French marriage had allied Scotland with the Catholic camp. The situation worsened when he died in 1542, leaving a young daughter, Mary, only a few days old, as his heir. The previous year his two young sons had both died. As he lay dying, he realised that the direct male line of Stuart Kings was at an end, "*It came wi' a lass* [Margery, Robert Bruce's daughter,] *and it will gang wi' a lass*" were his last words.

Henry VIII tried persuading Mary of Guise to agree to a marriage between the young Mary, Queen of Scots and his heir Prince Edward. When she refused, he launched an attack against Scotland in 1544, which, because it had the added ardour and hatred engendered when religious controversy was a factor, was ferocious and cruel. The looting, burning and killing was known as the 'Rough Wooing' and devastated a large area of the lowlands including Edinburgh. In 1547 the English army invaded again and defeated the Scots at the Battle of Pinkie, where Robert, fourteenth Laird's younger brother David was killed.

Despite the association of Protestantism with the English cause, the new religion continued to spread in Scotland. In an attempt to counter this, the Catholic cause was taken up with vigour by the Queen Mother, Mary of Guise, who acted as Regent for her infant daughter, and her chief adviser Cardinal Beaton, Archbishop of St Andrews. This ruthless and ambitious man personified all that good people of conscience and morality had against the Catholic hierarchy. He lead the life of a dissolute prince, living in splendid houses and maintaining a string of mistresses by whom he had eight illegitimate children. He attempted to retain the status quo, not by reforming the Catholic Church, but by bribery, fear and repression. Above all it was the way he dealt with his religious opponents that turned dislike to hatred.

In Scotland very few of the new Protestant preachers were burnt at the stake compared with England, but those who were so martyred had a deep effect on the population, the one directly opposite to that intended. In 1528 the reformer Patrick Hamilton was arrested and burnt at St Andrews. It was said *"the reek of Master Patrick Hamilton has affected as many as it blew upon"*[*]. In 1546 Cardinal Beaton arrested George Wishart, a native of Angus, tried him, and had him burnt for heresy, while he watched from his castle window. Two months later, a group of Protestants, including the young John Knox who had been a follower of George Wishart and was later to become the vociferous leader of the Reformed Church, broke into the castle and murdered the Cardinal.

The Catholic party still maintained the ascendancy under Mary of Guise, but after her death in 1560, the Protestants came to power and the first General Assembly was held. The Catholic Church had fallen, not through strong popular strength of feeling for the new religion, but rather through its own inability to reform. Once its authority was finally overthrown no one quite knew what form of Protestantism they wanted in Scotland.

It would be as well at this stage to describe the various religious factions whose bitter quarrels bedevilled the country for so many weary years. First there was the Roman Catholic hierarchy which had held power since the coming of feudalism and which was overthrown at the Reformation. The Protestants then

---

* The spot where Patrick Hamilton was burnt at St Andrews is marked with his initials "PH" set in the cobbles. A face may be seen, as if etched, on the wall above. It is said to have appeared there the morning after Patrick's death, and remained ever since. It was there the last time I looked.

took over first in England and then in Scotland. However within their ranks there were wide differences of opinion. They ranged from the high church adherents, who apart from refusing to accept the Pope's word as infallible, held to much the same form of worship as the Roman Catholics. The ritual, colourful vestments and the rule of bishops, which were believed to maintain the Apostolic Succession, the unbroken line of laying on of hands from the days of the Apostles and thus of Jesus Christ Himself, were still central. This group were called High Anglicans or Anglo-Catholics in England, and their way of worship eventually came under the wide umbrella of the established Church there. In Scotland they were called Episcopalians (from the Latin 'episcopus' *bishop*) and, because they were associated with the Stuart monarchy, they were to gain and lose power twice during the seventeenth century. They eventually lost out to the Presbyterians (from the Latin 'presbyter' *priest*) who became the established Church of Scotland. But even the Presbyterians had their factions and their quarrels grew worse as time went by. Each group thought that their way was the only right one and each believed God to be on their particular side; a dire recipe and one which left no room for compromise.

In 1560, when the Catholic Church fell from power, the Protestants in Scotland chose their preferred form of church government, which was Presbyterianism. They set up an assembly of ministers (clergy) and elders (laity) who had equal rights; there was no hierarchy. A Moderator was elected as leader for one year only. By around 1580 they had set up presbyteries which were local courts consisting of all the local ministers with one or two elders, again with an annually elected Moderator. Each parish had its kirk session of ruling elders who acted with the minister to enforce a strict discipline of morality. For the next three hundred years or more the Scots had to submit to their stern regime. A similar church government with an annual General Assembly exists in much the same form to this day in Scotland, though without the power that in times past dominated the lives of every citizen. Initially it was more moderate than it was to become. Even one of the most influential reformers, John Knox, advocated the idea of 'superintendents', who were bishops in all but name. It was only later in the next century, reacting to the efforts of Charles I to foist Episcopacy on Scotland, that the word 'bishop' developed a bad connotation to the Scots. It was then that the common name of that most prevalent of weeds, ground elder, became 'bishop's weed'. At the outset the Scottish Church was led by followers of Martin Luther, later the more extreme views of John Calvin were to prevail.

None the less, because of the deep corruption of the Catholic Church, anti-Catholic feeling ran high and wanton damage was inflicted on churches, with the cry "*Pull down the craws' nests, or the craws will build again*". Property, buildings, ornaments, books and anything that smacked of papacy was destroyed in an orgy of looting and burning. It was at this time that one such unruly mob descended upon Arbuthnott Kirk, and destroyed, among other things, the little images which were inset on the outside walls of the Arbuthnott Aisle, but the precious missal, prayer book and psalter had already been hidden away.

## Mary, Queen of Scots

Mary, Queen of Scots spent her childhood in France where she married the Dauphin, the heir to the French throne. For a short while she was Queen of France as well as Scotland. Then her young husband died and in 1561 she returned to Scotland to face the sharp contrast of climate and court life as well as the onslaught of the preaching of John Knox. Mary had a sweet disposition and initially coped well with her new situation; however she had an unerring knack for choosing the wrong husband. After two disastrous marriages she was forced to abdicate in favour of her infant son, James VI. She spent the last eighteen years of her life in prison in England, of which country she always maintained she was the rightful queen. Queen Elizabeth of England was considered to be illegitimate in the eyes of the Catholic Church, because she was the daughter of the divorced King Henry VIII and Ann Boleyn. Mary, through her descent from James IV and Margaret Tudor, was next in line and was the focus of many Catholic plots to depose Queen Elizabeth. Finally, after the failure of one such plot, Elizabeth reluctantly signed the death warrant of her cousin. Mary was executed at Fotheringay Castle in 1588. The two Queens never met.

## Robert, fourteenth Laird 1521-1579

Robert, fourteenth Laird succeeded his father (who had died after his pilgrimage to Amiens) in 1521. He was aged twelve and lived to seventy, so was laird for fifty-eight tumultuous years. It was during this time that the national religion changed from Roman Catholic to Protestant.

The Reverend Alexander Arbuthnot, chronicler of the fortunes of the family in the seventeenth century, tells of Robert's domestic life.

> *He was thrice honourably matched, first with the Laird of Dun Erskine his daughter; but she survived not long after, and left no issue behind her. After her decease, he married for his second wife Lady Christian Keith daughter of the Earl Marishal (who was killed at Flodden), a virtuous and worthy lady. He had by her numerous progeny of hopefull [promising] children, being four sons and six daughters. The eldest died a virgin, other two were married into the family of Carflogie, a daughter of which family this laird of Arbuthnott married for third wife.*

Robert first married at the age of sixteen in 1525. His bride was Katherine Erskine and although she tragically died within three years, Robert maintained a lifelong friendship with her brother John Erskine, the fifth Laird of Dun. Erskine was a prime mover in the establishment of the new Protestant religion. In 1527, while he was still under age, Robert got a dispensation from King James V granting him all the rights of his inheritance. Before the King died in 1542 Robert had a charter of confirmation from him for the lands at Arbuthnott as a Barony, still, nearly four hundred years since the establishment of feudalism, *"cum molendinis earundem"* (with the mill rights).

In 1544 Cardinal Beaton, thinking that in Robert, fourteenth Laird he had an ally in the son and grandson of staunch Catholics, granted him the Arbuthnott kirk-lands and the salmon-fishing rights that went with them. This was a reward for *"his zeal in combatting Lutherism and heresy throughout his domain"*. The grant was confirmed by the Crown on 10 February 1545. So after 340 years the Laird came into possession of the lands over which there had been so much contention between Duncan de Aberbothenoth and the Bishop of St Andrews. Any *"zeal against Lutheranism"* that Robert had was fast being eroded by growing disillusionment with the corrupt Catholic Church, and by the force of the new teaching. Therefore Cardinal Beaton's efforts to encourage him to sup-port the Catholic cause did not work. Just as when, one hundred years later, Charles I made an attempt to wean his great-great-grandson away from the Covenanters by creating him a Viscount, the Laird of Arbuthnott was not brought round. He took his reward but kept his own counsel.

The Roman Church had found that it was strictly in its interest to keep the majority of the laity in ignorance of the contents of the Bible and the true Gospel story; all learning and worship was conducted in Latin. However, despite persecution, men were preaching the new message and it was above all the general availability of the Bible, which came about through the invention of the printing press, that hastened the Reformation. Now bibles written in English were being smuggled in from England and the Continent.

It was possibly the capture and martyrdom of George Wishart in 1546 at the hands of Cardinal Beaton, the year after the grant of the kirklands, that was the turning point in persuading Laird Robert towards the Protestant cause. Wishart was a local man, a relation and protegee of the Laird's brother-in-law John Erskine, Laird of Dun. Erskine later entertained John Knox at his house, so Robert must have heard him preach and by the time of the first General Assembly in 1560, Robert took his place as an elder beside John Erskine who, despite his Protestant faith, was favoured by Mary, Queen of Scots. She pre-ferred to listen to him rather than other reformers, describing him as *"a mild and sweet-tempered man"*. Whatever his manner to the Queen, John Erskine had murdered a priest in his youth and has a reputation for violence still in Montrose where he instigated the burning down of the Blackfriars Monastery which contained a priceless library. However this was par for the course in those days.

Robert lived at Arbuthnott as Laird longer than any other. He lived through the fall of the power of the Roman Catholic Church and the English invasion by Henry VIII. On 13 March 1549, two years after the Battle of Pinkie where his brother David had been killed, Robert was directly involved in repulsing the English invasions. He received a letter from James, Earl of Arran, Governor of Scotland, asking him to join him in Edinburgh, where a force was being gath-ered in anticipation of another raid by the English.

Robert saw the coming and going of Mary, Queen of Scots. When the infant James VI became King in 1567, the Protestant religion had become well established in Scotland, with its distinct form of church government, the General Assembly. The next year Robert, in answer to a summons from the Regent Murray, attended Parliament in Edinburgh to show support for the King's party. As always when the monarch was a child there was even more strife among the feuding factions in Scotland.

The result of this continued instability was that society remained rigidly organised. Every man lived within a strict hierarchy with a superior to whom he owed allegiance. If a man broke the rules, he lost his place in the community. He was known as a 'broken man', one way out of his dilemma was to offer his services as a mercenary, usually ending up in the borders where warfare was a way of life. Such were the numbers of these men that during James VI's minority they were kept in custody around the country. In 1575 Laird Robert received a letter from the Regent Morton asking him to release one such man, called Tom Johnstone son of David of the Banks, and allow him to return home. The Arbuthnott parish was troubled by broken men again in 1664 and 1688. At Arbuthnott, the Laird felt sufficiently insecure to give priority to adding to the defences of his house. Robert enlarged the gatetower which would have given him a better view over the surrounding country.

1553 was an eventful year in the domestic life of Robert, fourteenth Laird. His second wife, Christian Keith, mother of ten of his children, died. He made over the running of the estate to his eldest son, Andrew, who on 7 August that year married Elizabeth Carnegie, daughter of Sir Robert Carnegie of Kinnaird. In the next month, September, with what seems surprising haste, Robert married his third wife Helen Clephane, who bore him eight more children.

In 1579 the Laird Robert went to stay at Findowrie with his son David, eldest son of his marriage to Helen Clephane. There he made out his will: "*In the first and befoir all thingis I leve my saule to Almichtie God Creator yrof my body to be bureit quhair* [where] *God plesis*". A modest request for one who had married three times, had eighteen children and managed to provide for each and every one of them through the judicious organisation of his property. Some of his descendants could have learnt from his canny management of his affairs.

Let us end the story of Robert, fourteenth Laird, by returning to the history of the Reverend Alexander Arbuthnot:

> *He had by his two worthy Ladies, viz. Ladie Christian Keith and*
> *Dam Helen Clepan eighteen sons and daughters which arrived*
> *to the perfect age of men and women and he saw them all*
> *(except Mr Robert and one daughter) honestly and honourably*
> *married in his own time, and bestowed on them large patri-*
> *monys without in the least diminution of his old estate, which*
> *he rather bettered.*

> *He sweetly and peaceably ended his days in the favour of God*

48

*and all good men, the 15th of October 1579, and was hon-
ourably interred in the Isle of Arbuthnot, builded by his grandfather of worthy memory, and left his eldest son Andrew to suc-
ceed him.*

## Principal Arbuthnott, 1538-1583

Principal Alexander Arbuthnott, as well as being the original chronicler of the
Arbuthnott family, was a key player in the establishment of the Presbyterian
Church in Scotland, so at this point let us take a small diversion from this
account of the lairds of the family to tell of the life of this admirable man.

Alexander Arbuthnott was the grandson of Robert, twelfth Laird, builder of the
Aisle and commissioner of the Missal. His father was the Laird's fifth son,
known as 'Andrew in Pitcarles' (the twelfth Laird having settled that property
on him). The Principal wrote with great affection of his father, who assisted
him with writing his Arbuthnott history. Andrew in Pitcarles *"lived as a widower for twenty-eight years in great chastity and brought up his children
with such honesty and diligence that it is difficult to know whether he made
a better father or mother to them. At last being an elderly man of seventy-
three years of age, having wisely settled the affairs of his household, he happily left this earthly life for the joys of Heaven."*

Principal Arbuthnott was educated firstly at St. Andrews and then at the age of
twenty-three he went to Bourges in France to study law. On his return to
Scotland he decided to take orders in the Reformed Church. In 1567 he started
to write his history of the Arbuthnott family entitled *"Originis et Incrementi
Arbuthnotticae Familiae Descriptio Historica."* It was translated from Latin
into Scots by W Morison, the minister at Benholm. This history is a source of
invaluable information without which our knowledge of early family history
would be very hazy indeed.

In 1567 the young Alexander was presented by Robert, fourteenth Laird, as
minister at Arbuthnott (the laird had the right to choose the incumbent of the
parish). A year later he was called by the General Assembly to examine a book
called *The Fall of the Roman Church*, in which the king was described as
*"Head of the Church"*. This matter brought him headlong into a conflict which
became the main reason for James VI's antipathy for him in particular and the
Reformed Church in general, and proved to be a bone of contention which
reached its final crisis in the time of Charles I. The Church insisted that the
king was not the head or governor of the Church, (as Queen Elizabeth was in
England). Their doctrine insisted that they had *"but one King, Our Lord Jesus
Christ"*. This was the view that the Principal was expected to enforce. Having
read the book and found the offending passages, Alexander ordered Bassendyne
the printer to recall all copies that he had printed and told him to sell no more
until the objectionable passage had been removed. He was also to remove a
*"profane song"* which was printed at the end of an edition of the book of
psalms. Bassendyne was not to print any other book without the licence of the

*St. Ternan from the 15th century missal illuminated by James Sibbald, who diplomatically gave the saint the face of his superior, the Archbishop of St Andrews*

*The Jacobite Laird, John, 5th Viscount, "a man of strict honour and very religious, but not otherwise possessed of great mental endowments"*

*Jean Morrison, wife of the 5th Viscount, painted as a pair to her husband just after they married in defiance of her father in 1714. Passion cooled and they later lived in separate wings of the house.*

*Robert Keith, 15th Viscount of Arbuthnott, at Argenta Gap, Italy. His distinguished record in two World Wars has given the family one of its more important historical figures.*

Supreme Magistrate and any book on religion would have to be checked by the Assembly's commission. With such fierce censorship, the Principal must have had great ardour for his cause to be chosen to carry out the task of rooting out this seditious material. The pitfalls experienced by Bassendyne in printing a book and falling foul of the church authorities may have prompted him to take on a relation of the Principal, another Alexander Arbuthnot, as his partner. In 1575 they were appointed printers to the King and were issued with a licence to print the Bible, the first in Scotland[*].

By 1569, John Erskine, then Superintendent of Angus and the Mearns, appointed him as first Protestant Principal of King's College, Aberdeen, having expelled the previous incumbent for "*adherence to Popery*". He was chosen as Moderator of the General Assembly of the Reformed Church in 1573, 1577 and 1578. A stone in the wall by the pulpit at Arbuthnott Kirk commemorates his first appointment as Moderator. It has the initials 'AA AR' and the date '1573' carved on it.

The Principal was regarded not only as one of the great scholars and mathematicians of his day, but as a renowned poet. The Principal's decision to place his loyalty to his Church before his duty to his King could not have been an easy one. His dilemma is expressed through his poems. Three of them are part of a collection of Scottish poetry in the care of the Pepys Library of Magdalene College, Cambridge. One of them eloquently tells of the dilemma of living in those times and the conflicts of loyalty to family, faith and to his King, who deserved his allegiance but only after obedience had been rendered to his God.

> *Under my God, I wald obey my prince;*
> *Bot civile weir dois sa trouble the cais,*
> *That scarcelie wait I quham to reverence;*
> *Quhat till eschew, or quhat for till embrace.*
> *Our nobils now sa fickil ar, alace!*
> *This day thai say, the morne thai will repent.*
> *Quhat marvel is thoch I murne and lament?*
>
> *Fainewald I leif in concord, and in peice;*
> *Without divisioun, rancour, or debait.*
> *Bot now, alace! in every land and place*
> *The fyr of hatrent kindlit is so hait,*
> *That cheretie doth ring in nane estait;*
> *Thoch all concur to hurt the innocent.*
> *Quhat marvel is thoch I murne and lament?*
>
> *I luif justice; and wald that everie man*
> *Had that quhilk richtlie dois to him perteine;*
> *Yet all my kyn, allya, or my clan,*
> *In richt or wrang I man alwayis mantene,*

---

[*] See Appendix 2 for an account of the career of Alexander Arbuthnot, printer.

*I maun applaud, quhen thai thair matters mene,*
*Thoch conscience thairto do not consent,*
*Quhat marvel is thoch I morne and lament?*

Another poem called *The Praises of Wemen* has the lines

*To man obedient*
*Evin lyk ane willie wand.*
*Bayth faythfull and fervent,*
*Ay reddie at command.*\*

It seems he never found this ideal woman, he remained a batchelor.

The young James VI was brought up within a strict regime, controlled by his fierce tutor George Buchanan, who with his other guardians determined that the Protestant faith should be upheld. They prejudiced him against his mother, and put him through a thorough and arduous education. When he finally took power into his own hands, he had a deep mistrust of those who had kept him under their control. Among them were the leaders of the Protestant Church. In his book, the *Basilikon Doron*, in which he set out his views on the art of kingship for his son, of the Church he said "*never rose a faction in the time of my minority, no trouble sen-syne* [since], *but they were upon the wrong end of it*". Uppermost in his mind, no doubt, was the approval by the General Assembly in 1582 of the Raid of Ruthven when the young King was kidnapped. The abduction separated him from the influence of his beloved cousin, the Duke of Lennox, who, it was rightly feared, was persuading him towards Catholicism.

The Principal was ordered by an Act of the Assembly to go to St. Andrews where he had been appointed minister. King James VI, then aged eighteen and newly escaped from the captivity in which he had been kept for nearly a year after the Raid of Ruthven, was also in St Andrews, trying to establish his authority. He, fearful of the influence of the Principal on the Assembly, forbade him to leave Aberdeen. If he disobeyed he would be "*put to the horn*" or outlawed. The Assembly protested at the King's high-handed behaviour, but he remained adamant. Principal Alexander never recovered from the blow of incurring the King's displeasure and he died soon after on 16 October 1583.

It is to Principal Arbuthnott that we possibly owe the preservation of the illuminated manuscripts commissioned by Robert, twelfth Laird. In 1580, at a time when church inspectors were sent round to see that folk were abiding by the "*true faith*" and not harbouring "*papist relics*", the Principal was appointed by the commissaries in Edinburgh as one of the commissioners to examine the papers at Arbuthnott House.

---

\* See Appendix 3 for a translation of the Principal's poems into modern English.

*Cognition taken by Mr. Alexander Arbuthnott, Principal of the
College of Aberdeen, Paul Frazer Chanter of Brechin, and others, commissionaries of Edinburgh, to examine the writs and
evidents then in the house of Arbuthnott and to make an inventory of the same. Wherupon they put certain writs respecting
the liferent of Helen Clephan, relict [widow] of Robert
Arbuthnott of that Ilk, into a Flanders chest in the wardrobe
room, and delivered the key to Alexander Bishop of Brechin,
then husband of the said Helen, the said chest and writs to
remain in the house of Arbuthnott for her behoof, and Andrew
Arbuthnott then of that ilk to permit access to them on security
that they be replace, further the said commissioners put the
writs and evidences respecting the said Andrew of Arbuthnott
into the Charter Chest and delivered to him the key thereof.*

*Dated at Arbuthnott, 6 February 1580.*

It is most likely that at this point the Principal knew the whereabouts of his
grandfather's illuminated books and chose not to destroy them.

## Andrew, fifteenth Laird 1579-1606

In 1553 Robert, fourteenth Laird, while retaining a life rent, handed over the
management of the estate to his eldest son, Andrew. This practice of handing
over the estate to the heir, once he is experienced enough to manage it, has
been kept up throughout the generations, even when, as in the case of the
childless sixteenth Laird, the heir was a nephew and not a son. Another practice of the family which was particularly successful in the time of Robert, fourteenth laird and for the next three generations was that of acquiring lands and,
with those already incorporated in the barony, to grant them to other members
of the family. In feudal law a landowner could 'sub-feft' (sub-let), his land to
tenants usually for an initial fee and an annual rent or 'feu'. The landowner
remained 'superior' of the lands, with the right to regain them in the event of
non-payment or some other offence, when there was no direct heir or during
the period the inheritor was a minor. (The king had the same right to regain
the running of a holding when inherited by a minor). Close relations of the
laird therefore lived nearby, even in the parish of Arbuthnott itself. They were
a support in running the church as ministers or elders. They were occasionally
called on to be the guardian of a laird while he was a child and to run the estate
for him, when they were given the title Tutor of Arbuthnott.

Andrew, fifteenth Laird married Elizabeth Carnegie in 1553, the year he took
over management of the estate. They had five children. He succeeded his
father as Laird in 1579 and probably met King James VI the next year.
Andrew's mother, Christian Keith, was sister to the Earl Marshal who lived at
Dunnottar Castle. In April 1580, James VI stayed at Dunnottar Castle while on
one of his progresses through the country. Later that year Andrew agreed that
his eldest son, Robert, should accompany his cousin, the Master of Marshal, to

attend the young King at court*1. The following year young Robert married the Master's sister, Mary Keith, once again uniting the two families. Through his mother, Christian Keith, Andrew could claim descent from James I, and therefore a double descent from Joan Beaufort, since he was also descended from her through his grandmother, Jean Stewart. He was thus directly descended from both the Scottish and English royal lines.

Andrew received at least five letters from King James VI. In 1583, the King sent him a letter asking him for reassurance of his loyalty and support and in 1588, Andrew was summoned to Edinburgh to take part in a Convention of Nobles, Lairds and Burghers. However it was financial help that the King needed most, especially for the expenses incurred by his marriage to Anne of Denmark, when he wished to greet his new Queen with suitable ceremony*2. The King was under such financial strictures that he had, at one time, to borrow a pair of stockings from the Earl of Mar in order to be adequately dressed to receive the Spanish Ambassador. All this changed when, in 1603, Queen Elizabeth I of England died and James inherited the English crown.

Elizabeth Carnegie had died in 1563 and Andrew married as his second wife, Margaret Hoppringal, widow of John Erskine, son of the fifth Laird of Dun. They had no children. The Erskines of Dun were at that time having to support four dependent ladies, one of them was Margaret Hoppringal who had a life rent for a yield of some of the land, even though she had remarried. To pay for these ladies the Erskines sold land to their neighbours:

> *Part of the lands of Arrat and Lichtonhill in the Lordship of Brechin were bought from Erskine of Dun by Andrew Arbuthnott of Arbuthnott* [fifteenth Laird] *for his third son James in 1591 for 15,000 merks and the remaining portion was acquired by Sir Robert Arbuthnott of that ilk* [sixteenth Laird] *in 1611.*

The Reverend Alexander Arbuthnot is fulsome in his praise for the Laird Andrew. *"This Andrew was an excellent son of an excellent father for by his honest industry and prudent management of his affairs he augmented his fortune very much."* The Reverend Alexander then goes on to describe how Andrew put all the family affairs in good order, and describes an incident when a tenant forfeited the right to his property through illegally taking lands from another. Andrew as his superior had the right to reclaim the property and was advised to do so by his friends. However Andrew who *"never did the least act of injustice and oppression to any .... asked them if he had ever paid money for that land, they answered no; then said he, I will never possess that for which I paid not the just value and after he had sent for the man, and convinced him of his error, he dismissed him with a new holding of his land"*

---

*1. See Appendix 4 for a transcription of the letter from the Master of Marshal
*2. See Appendix 5 for one of these letters, requesting supplies against the arrival of the Queen.

The wise old Laird died in March 1606, leaving his son Robert to inherit the estate. He was buried in the Arbuthnott Aisle. Three years before his death, James VI had inherited the English throne and moved his court down to London.

### *Robert, sixteenth Laird 1606-1631 and Robert, seventeenth Laird 1631-1633*

Robert, sixteenth Laird continued to increase and unite the lands of Arbuthnott. He was knighted in 1609 and may well have travelled to London to be knighted personally by the King, whom he had attended as a young man. His marriage to Mary Keith was childless. His heir was his nephew Robert, the son of his younger brother, James, who had been given the lands of Arrat by their father Andrew, fifteenth Laird. The sixteenth Laird took great pains to have his heir groomed for his role through education and travel, as reported in *The Scots Peerage*:

> *Through his uncle's care he had received a liberal education, not only at home, but abroad, for in 1611 a license under the signet was granted to Robert Arbuthnott of Arrat to repair to France and other foreign countries, and there to remain for five years 'for the better training up of himself in suche good and virteous exercise as becometh one of his qualitie', on condition always that during his absence he behave himself loyally and do nothing prejudicial to the true religion.*

Clearly there was to be no sowing of wild oats while he was abroad. Robert returned to Scotland by 1615, in which year he married Lady Margaret Keith, a relative of his aunt's, who died soon afterwards. It is not clear whether she was still alive in 1616, when Robert was travelling again, this time to London where he purchased a new coach.

It is difficult to distinguish between the roles played by the sixteenth and seventeenth Lairds in the running of the Arbuthnott estates. Both were called Robert and both were knighted, and therefore referred to in contemporary documents as 'Sir Robert', which adds to the confusion. It seems that Robert, sixteenth Laird formally handed everything over in 1616 to his nephew, who in effect became the Laird in his uncle's lifetime, although his uncle was to live for another fifteen years. He was even referred to as 'Robert, Laird of Arbuthnott, younger'. After the death of Margaret Keith, he married as his second wife Margaret Fraser, daughter of Lord Lovat, in April 1617. In the summer of that year James VI made his only return visit to Scotland after he became monarch of the two kingdoms.

In 1619 Mary, Lady Arbuthnott, wife of the sixteenth Laird, died. It must have been a source of great sadness that although both these lairds married Keith ladies neither had any children by them. Mary left her jewellry to "*the Ladies of Arbuthnot her successors*" and her clothing "*for the favour she has to the noble house of Marischal, from which she is descended, and the love she bears her dearest nephew and his lady, my Lord and my Lady Keith, she bequeaths to his eldest daughter, Lady Mary Keith, whom failing, her sister, a gown of black satin and certain other articles of clothing and chains of pearls, with 4,000 merks to be paid at her marriage".*

Nothing was done to improve the amenities at Arbuthnott House during the first half of the seventeenth century, it remained the battlemented castle built by Robert, twelfth Laird. Times remained contentious and the situation was to become very much worse, leading to civil war. The sixteenth and seventeenth Lairds had to concentrate on keeping their dwelling in a defensive mode. Local quarrels were still settled by violent means; neighbouring landowners spoiled for a fight. The laird of Arbuthnott was by this time a powerful man owning large stretches of land both in Angus and the Mearns. He was not without his enemies and still needed the support of his relatives. The other families involved in two such disputes were near neighbours and had in times past been related by marriage to the Arbuthnott family. One quarrel was with the Strachans of Thornton. A daughter of this house had married Andrew in Pitcarles, son of Robert, twelfth Laird and was thus the mother of Principal Arbuthnott. The Privy Council made a judgement on the case in 1616:

> *The Lords of Council, understanding that there is a quarrel between Sir Robert Arbuthnot of that Ilk and Strachan of Thornton anent the teinds of some lands, and that the King's Peace will be broken, order these parties to find caution in ten thousand merks each to keep the peace.*

Archibald Mason, schoolmaster at Arbuthnott from 1883-1913 tells of another dispute:

> *The Wisharts of Pitarrow and the Arbuthnotts were not on friendly terms for it is recorded in 1629 Luke Simpson messenger of arms was sent by Sir Robert to Wishart of Pitarrow on some important errand but Wishart gave Luke "ane kuff for the Laird of Arbuthnot his maister's sake and another for the discharge of his office". For this Wishart was fined 1000 merks and "warded in the tolbooth".*

In an earlier incident in 1607, Sir John Wishart of Pitarrow and his brother James Wishart of Balfeich were required by the court "*not to carry hagbuts or pistolets hereafter*" after they had harried some of the Laird of Arbuthnott's tenants. These Wisharts were no doubt descendants of George Wishart, burnt to death by Cardinal Beaton in 1546. Relations must have deteriorated badly between the two families since the 1460s when Margaret Wishart married Robert, twelfth Laird as his first wife.

Robert, seventeenth Laird played a prominent role in national and local affairs. The register of the Privy Council noted in 1623 that Sir Robert Arbuthnott "*was appointed a commissioner to England to treat respecting the export thither of all Scottish Woll* [wool] *not draped and wrought it at home"* he was *"written for to attend Council anent the establishment of manufactories"*. He was therefore given charge of the export of wool and the organisation of the Scottish wool trade. He was also appointed Justice of the Peace and convener for Kincardineshire.

We have a picture then of a prominent figure, well educated, honoured with a knighthood, powerful and respected. His career was described by the Reverend Alexander Arbuthnot in the flowery language of his time:

> *He was without disparagement every way both in body and mind one of the best accomplished gentlemen, not only that governed that family but in the whole kingdom, of a stately, comely personage, and of courteous affable behaviour (for he was well educated abroad in France) he was most hospitable both to friends and strangers, and many times he nobly entertained the greatest peers of the nation in his house; his own private affairs he dextrously managed with much prudence and was capable by reason of his singular qualifications of the greatest public trust, and among the rest of his many rare natural endowments, he had a gift of expressing himself with such a torrent of unaffected eloquence, that he was admired by all that knew him, and always chosen by the rest of the Barons to be their mouth before the highest Courts of the Kingdom in a word he put such a lustre upon his family by his splendid virtues and worthy actions that all about him courted his favour and friendship and he became to be as singly esteemed as most of his rank and quality, and certainly if God had not removed him to a better life by untimely death in the midst of his days he had done great things for his family, for being subject to gout and stone* [gallstones], *the last of these diseases cut his days.*

Sadly the seventeenth Laird became ill in the prime of his life. He only out-lived his uncle by two years, his death in 1633 ended an illustrious career. His young son Robert became eighteenth Laird while still under fifteen years of age. Both the funeral orations were given by John Sibbald, for thirty years minister of Arbuthnott Kirk.

This John Sibbald was a great-grandson of Robert Arbuthnott, fourteenth Laird, and was the minister at Arbuthnott from 1626-1662. He saw to it that a school was built, giving money towards the building work (the General Assembly in 1642 had ordered that there should be a school in every parish). When he died he left money both for a salary for the schoolmaster and for the poor of the parish. He left his valuable collection of books to augment the library already started by Principal Arbuthnott, which were kept in the priest's room on the first floor of the Arbuthnott Aisle in the kirk and which finally disappeared when the last few volumes were found rotting away in the nineteenth century.

*The redoubtable Lady Margaret Fraser, mother of the 1st Viscount, and second wife of Robert, 17th Laird. She took a comfortable number of possessions with her to her new husband at Gleneagles even if she did fail to impoverish the Arbuthnott estate by claiming a widow's terce in 1635.*

## Robert, first Viscount and eighteenth Laird 1633-55

There is some question as to whether Robert, eighteenth Laird, was the son of his father's first or second marriage. Since both wives were called Margaret, the confusion is difficult to unravel. Writing in the 1920s, Mrs P S-M Arbuthnot puts forward the theory in her *Memories of the Arbuthnots of Kincardineshire and Aberdeenshire* that he was son of Margaret Keith, not Margaret Fraser. Margaret Fraser certainly behaved more like a step-mother than a mother. There is a portrait of her with the initials DMF for Dame Margaret Fraser painted in the background, painted in 1666 after she had been widowed for a second time. Her likeness to Robert the eighteenth Laird, who became the first Viscount, is evident. She has the same dark eyes.

Whatever the truth, she had no scruples in impoverishing the new Laird's estate by bleeding the assets to support her second husband, the Laird of Gleneagles, whose estate in Perthshire had fallen on hard times. We will return to the Reverend Alexander Arbuthnot to tell the story:

*He being young when his father died, the fortune (though under the administration of his uncle James) had sustained great loss which was occasioned by the means of his mother after his father's death having married Hadden of Glenygies [Gleneagles] whose family had fallen with great decay. By impoverishing....the family of Arbuthnot, he resolved to raise his own. For his father and granduncle having conquested several Baronies of a considerable value as was before narrated, and his mother not being expressly excluded in contract matrimonial from a Terce (as our countrymen call it) the said Laird of Glenygies her second husband taking advantage of this, pur-*

*sued the heir and his Tutor for a Terce of the whole conquest of lands .*

As well as making this unjustified claim for a terce from the estate, Margaret Fraser seems to have taken considerable property with her when she left Arbuthnott to join her new husband. Among the Arbuthnott Papers is an inventory of expenses incurred when Lady Arbuthnott needed transport to take her from "*ye ludging of Bervie to ye boat to Gordon*", where she embarked with

*Imprimis 3 trunk ane gryt gilt flanderis coffer; Item of Lifts litle & mekle xiii; Ane mekle Flanders croill, lokit; Item ane caboneit for wtt keping ane nyt sellar*

*Firstly 3 trunks: One great gilt Flanders coffer, Eight small and large pieces of luggage, One large locked Flanders trunk, one chest containing a large quantity of silver items.*

She left Gourdon by boat with these and various bundles of bedding, household linen and gowns in May 1635. The Flanders coffer may have been the one in which documents were locked after the visit of Principal Arbuthnott in 1580. In 1636 a judgement, handed down in favour of her son, stated that because Margaret had remarried, no terce was due. In the Reverend Alexander's words, her "*design was utterly blasted*". It seems unlikely, however, that any of the items she took with her were ever returned.

After the death of their father, Robert and his brothers and sisters came under the care of their uncle James, as Tutor of Arbuthnott, but the arrangement was not to last long. The Reverend Alexander described James' tragic death:

*James was drowned in the North Esk: For crossing the North Esk on horse, and his footman behind him when it had over- flowed and swelled above its ordinary channel and was some- what frozen, the horse stumbling, and thereby his footman behind him, falling from his horse, pulled his master off with him, and not being able by reason of his cloak and other furni- ture, and with the impetuousness of the river to recover himself, he there perished, which painful blow did extremely affect his relatives and acquaintances.*

The young eighteenth Laird had experienced the loss of his popular and talent- ed father, as well as the acrimonious court case against his mother and now he was deprived of the advice and care of his uncle. A mark of the seventeenth century was that all the lairds lived comparatively short lives and died while their sons were still young. In this they echo the pattern of the kings of Scotland in the previous century. While the Arbuthnotts did not die violent deaths, they lived in extremely stressful times, when life was hazardous and medical care was still primitive. It is surprising how much they managed to achieve in their short lives.

# Chapter 6

## Crown or Covenant

Robert, eighteenth Laird was to become the first Viscount. He lived in the traumatic time of Charles I and the Protectorate under Cromwell after the Civil War.

When the two Kingdoms of England and Scotland were joined and James VI moved to London, he found life a great deal more comfortable. He only returned to Scotland once during the rest of his life. He ruled from a distance but since he knew his nobles and officials well, he managed skillfully to play them off against each other, and since he was at last at a safe distance from their feuding, he could deal with them firmly. He had a first hand knowledge of his Scottish subjects and the shrewdness to know how to deal with them, and although he must have advised his son, Charles did not inherit his father's subtlety.

Charles I's reign in Scotland was no more successful than it was south of the border where it was marked with continued and deepening controversy over religion. In the days of Principal Arbuthnott the Scots had achieved the church government they wanted with a General Assembly meeting regularly and dictating the running of the Church. However both James VI and Charles I regarded this church government as a threat to their power, and seldom allowed the Assembly to meet. They regarded the monarchy as supreme. Charles especially believed passionately in the 'Divine Right of Kings'. This doctrine maintained that the monarch had supreme power from God and that all government, of both Church and State must come through the King. Charles was totally immovable on this point and brought on civil war and his own execution because he would not bow to the idea that Parliament, or indeed, the Scottish Church, had any right to make their own decisions. The divine state of the monarchy was endorsed, in Charles' view, by a remarkable power he had, known as 'The King's Touch' by which he could cure scrofula, a skin ailment, by laying his hand on the sufferer. Charles I had, to a marked degree, the Stuart character. He combined personal dignity and charm, which inspired the passionate loyalty of his followers, with a total incapacity to understand or judge the feelings of his subjects.

Men of conscience were again in a tragic dilemma. The King's views ran in direct conflict with the Presbyterian ideal which professed that God and not the King was their sole authority. There was an inevitable clash. Charles' insistence on having bishops and all the trappings of High Anglican rites at his Coronation at St. Giles shocked the Presbyterian Scots. This was followed the next year by the imposition of a Prayer Book, which the King insisted be read in every kirk in the kingdom. This was anathema to the Presbyterians who ordained that the Bible only was the basis of their services and advocated extempore prayers. Riots followed, during one of which occurred a famous incident when Jenny Geddes heaved a stool at the minister in St Giles Cathedral. The Bishop of Brechin thought it wise to stand in the pulpit with two primed pistols in front of him while he read from the Prayer Book. It was all too much for the protagonists of the Reformed Church; in 1638 they drew up the 'National Covenant', which, while it did not challenge the King's power, insisted on a return to the *"true religion"*, Presbyterianism. The young Laird of Arbuthnott was among the majority who supported it, who became known as 'Covenanters'.

*Robert Arbuthnott, 18th Laird was granted the title of Viscount of Arbuthnott by Charles I in a vain attempt to buy the loyalty of this staunch Presbyterian.*

When Charles I came to Scotland in 1641, he gave out various honours in a final desperate attempt to gain support for his cause. He must have thought that the young Robert Arbuthnott, although he was a Covenanter, could be won round coming as he did from a family that had supported the Stuarts well in the past. The King therefore created him Viscount of Arbuthnott and Lord of (*"Dominus de"*) Bervie. This was to no avail. When civil war broke out soon afterwards in England, Lord Arbuthnott remained with the Covenanters, who allied themselves with Parliament as the Army of the Covenant.

In 1644 the first Viscount went to Aberdeen with 500 armed followers in support of the cause, their motto was "*For the Covenant, Religionne, the Croun and Kingdome*". They seemed still to hope to combine their religious convictions with loyalty to the Crown.

Meantime that brilliant but unstable star, the Marquis of Montrose, took centre stage. He had initially supported the Covenant, and had even been in prison during the King's visit in 1641, but when he saw the Covenant supporters taking up arms in support of the Parliamentarians, he determined to win Scotland back for the King. He assembled a Royalist army and conducted a quick and devastatingly successful campaign. By the spring of 1645 he and his victorious forces were sweeping through the Mearns. Lord Keith, the Earl Marshal was besieged in Dunnottar, along with sixteen ministers, who no doubt stiffened his resolve, and could not be persuaded by Montrose to take up the royalist cause. Montrose in his anger ordered the destruction of the surrounding countryside. Among his forces were Highlanders and Irishmen over whom he had either no inclination or little will to keep control. Far from their own countryside, flushed with drink and the power of victory, they looted, burned and slaughtered animals and people alike. Stonehaven was destroyed and the army swept through the lands of Arbuthnott. Only the house itself escaped devastation. Civil war cruelly divides families, but about the time of the Covenant, Robert, eighteenth Laird had married Lady Marjorie Carnegie. Lady Arbuthnott and Lady Montrose were sisters, both daughters of the Earl of Southesk. This fact may have spared the house itself from burning. The episode left a legacy of hatred against the royalist cause, not least with the Viscount himself.

A description of the dreadful destruction wrought in the district by Montrose's army was given at the time:

> *It is said the people of Stonehaven and Cowie came out, men and women, children at their feet, and children in their arms, crying howling and weeping, praying the Earl [Marshal] for God's cause to save them from this fire as soon as it was kindled. But the poor people got no answer, nor knew they where to go with their children. Lamentable to see. Fetteresso was also fired and a quarter of it burnt; but the whole low building and cornyards utterly destroyed and burnt up. They fired the pleasant park of Fetteresso. Some trees burnt, but others being green could not burn well. But the hart, the hind, the deer, the roe screamed at the sight of the fire; but they were all taken and slain. The horses, mares, oxen and cows were all likewise killed; and the whole Barony of Dunnottar and Fetteresso utterly spoilt, plundered and undone. After this he marche to Drumlithie and Urie, pertaining to John Forbes of Leslie the great covenanter. He fired the place, burning all the vaults, together with the low buildings, corn and cornyards; and he plundered the whole ground. He sent to his own brother-in-law, the Viscount of Arbuthnott; but as he said by his order, there was burnt and plundered to him about 24 pleuchis of land.*

In 1649 Lord Arbuthnott made a claim of four thousand pounds for damages wrought to his estate by Montrose claiming *"his Landis was not only destroyed and waisted by burning the haill houses and cornes, but tenantis and servandis wes most cruelly murderit"*. He got his compensation and was given exemption from a levy for *"horse and foote"*.

The Royalist cause was doomed, their army was defeated in England and the King was captured, Montrose went into exile. Oliver Cromwell, leader of the Parliamentarians, was in Edinburgh in 1648 and summoned Lord Arbuthnott to a meeting. A witness of the time wrote:

> *While Cromwell remained at the Canongate those that haunted him most, were, besides the Marquis of Argyle, Loudoun the Chancellor, the Earl of Lothian, the Lords Arbuthnot, Elcho and Burleigh and of the Ministers Mr David Dickson, Mr Robert Blair and Mr James Guthrie. What passed between them, cannot be known infallibly, but it was talked very loud that he did communicate to them his design in reference to the King and had their assent thereto.*

There is no doubt that the first Viscount was extreme in his religious views but whether he condoned the execution of Charles I, we do not know. The only documentary evidence of his religious practice is the granting in 1642 of a licence to eat meat in Lent. Even then, eighty years after the overthrow of the Catholic Church, the habit of fasting was still with the Scots, in fact with the resurgence of a Calvinistic attitude which came with the Covenanters, such abstinence was deemed worthy. Another factor in the maintenance of the tradition of abstaining from meat and the eating of fish on Friday and in Lent was the lobby of fish merchants, who strove to maintain such a tradition by law, for fear of losing their livelihood.

By the time of the King's execution in London in 1649, the Presbyterians had split into two groups, the 'Engagers' and the 'Resolutioners'. In 1647 the Engagers had struck up a bargain with Charles I, getting his word that he would impose Presbyterianism in England for three years, if they supported him against the Parliamentarians. The Resolutioners were bitterly opposed to any compromise. In January 1649, they sat in their first Kirk Party Parliament. Lord Arbuthnott was one of only sixteen nobles to take part. They set about purging the kirk of any who had taken part in the 'Engagement'.

At Arbuthnott Kirk those who had supported the Engagement were made publicly to repent. *"The said day Thomas Allades tutor of that ilk, Mr David Sibbald of Kair and Robert Raitt in Mickle Fiddes, 'Engagers' who a good while before that had humbled themselves before the presbytery for the corruption and that offense by the sustaining of the unlawful act of Parliament did the like before the congregation upon their knees and subscribed the oath affecting the unlawfulness of the said Engagement"*. This was only four years after the destruction wrought by Montrose in the name of the King, perhaps that explains the unpleasant scene that this account conjures up. It also exposes a streak of ruthlessness in the character of the first Viscount, who must have been present at this public humiliation of his neighbours.

When Cromwell and the other regicides decided to execute King Charles, most Scots were horrified and turned their allegiance to his son, Charles II. The Covenanters who had sided with the Parliamentarians in the Civil War had done so because they were promised the freedom to practice their religion as they wanted and not because they wished the King personal harm. War broke out again in a bid to restore the new young King to the throne, but Cromwell's army by then was invincible and by 1651 Scotland was under an army of occupation.

The first Viscount was made a Privy Councillor. He attended the General Assembly in 1650 and 1651. That year his first wife, Marjorie Carnegie died, they had married in 1639 and had had a son and a daughter. In 1653 he married Katherine Fraser, they also had a boy and a girl. They embarked on improvements to the house. An extra floor was added to the south wing of the house, above the drawing room, and their initials were carved on a stone above their bedroom window.

Katherine Fraser seems to have been the subject of country gossip and the *Fraser Papers* quote an unflattering story told of her by John Napier, a tenant of the neighbouring estate of Allardice in the 1750s. He was speaking of times one hundred years before his own.

> *The 2nd wife of the 1st Lord was a daughter of Lord Lovat. She was extremely extravagant and oppressive to the tenants and almost occasioned the ruin of the Arbuthnott family. She is still mentioned with disrespect in the country under the appellation given her in her life time from the dress she wore of 'Lady Green gowns'*

It seems likely that these stories have been erroneously attached to Katherine Fraser. John Napier has confused her with her kinswoman and mother-in-law, Margaret Fraser, widow of the seventeenth Laird, who so unscrupulously filled her coffers before leaving Arbuthnott twenty years earlier.

Only two years after his marriage to Katherine Fraser, on 10 October 1655 the first Viscount died while still in his early forties. His contemporary, the Laird of Brodie, wrote in his diary "*I have heard of the death of Lord Arbuthnott and desired to be unfeignedly humbled by this loss. He was the shadow to honest people in these places and shall we not look on it as a publick strok or a marke of God's anger*". Those who had suffered from his inflexibility, for example the Engagers who had had to repent publicly, cannot have felt the same. What might have been the fate of the first Viscount had he lived until after the Restoration of the monarchy in 1660, is difficult to assess. He had thrown in his lot with the hard core of Covenanters. He had supported the

Marquis of Argyll, the leader of the faction opposed to 'The Engagement'. In 1661, a year after the restoration of Charles II to the throne, Argyll was taken south to London, put on trial and executed for his co-operation with the Cromwellian Government. Robert, first Viscount's death may have been timely. He had espoused extreme religious and political views and pursued them publicly. Through his direct involvement in the fate of Scotland, he left a legacy of lands ravaged by the royalist army but at least an undamaged house and a Viscountcy.

### Robert, second Viscount and nineteenth Laird
### 1655-1682 "the Wise Lord"

When Robert, second Viscount inherited from his father in 1655 at the age of fifteen, the whole of Scotland was under military rule. After Charles I was executed the sympathy of the Scots went to his son, the young King Charles II, who came to Scotland in a vain effort to regain the throne. He was crowned at Scone and stayed at Dunnottar Castle, but the New Model Army that Cromwell had forged out of years of battle came north and succeeded in defeating all opposition. Scotland was occupied. The local army headquarters was at Dunnottar which, in 1652, fell to the Cromwellian army after an eight month siege. Surrender was inevitable once Cromwell had brought his artillery on to the Black Hill opposite the castle. The site where it stood is today marked by a pillared monument, easily seen from the modern road.

While Cromwell's army occupied Scotland it enjoyed a free range of the perks of the land. A letter written by Colonel Lilburne, the English Commander-in-Chief, to the officer in command at Dunnottar, gives an idea of how they spent their time:

> *Sir - Haveing formerly writt to you to preserve the breede of hawkes neere to Dunnottyr Castle, I desire you to give order to the man that clymbes the rockes that hee doe nott dispose or give away any of the hawkes to any person whatsoever, without particular direction from your selfe, and that you will cause him to preserve them for me, and that you will doe me the favour to send to the Lord Arbuthnott's Fawkner to come for them about the time they are readie, that he may bring them unto your very true friend.*

The English army officers obviously enjoyed the sport of falconry and appropriated both the falcons and their falconers.

The Keith family, the Earls Marshal, continued to live at Dunnottar, despite its occupation by troops. In 1658 the young Robert Arbuthnott, second Viscount, then aged eighteen, was taken there by his cousin Lord Southesk, to pay his respects to the Lady Elizabeth Keith, daughter of the Earl Marshal. An extract from the *Fraser Papers* tells the story:

*It seems this Viscount's appearance was so inviting that the
young lady fell deeply in love with him at first sight, and tho'
the Earl saw that his finances were embarrassed, yet he was so
pleased with the young man's appearance that he readily
agreed to the match.*

After this auspicious start, their marriage should have been a happy one. The
reference to the poor state of the young Laird's finances may suggest that the
incursions of Montrose's army had been a severe blow to the income of the
Arbuthnott estates despite the payment of compensation. The Lady Elizabeth
Keith died in 1664, leaving a son, Robert, who was baptised on 8 October 1661
and a daughter, Margaret, who between them were to produce thirty-two children. In 1667, Robert married, as his second wife, Katherine Gordon and had
four more sons and four daughters. He chose wisely despite initial doubts as to
her suitability, which he expressed in a letter to his cousin:

*I am very confident the gentlewomane is of ane good disposi-
tione and fears God (although a Gordon), and her many
friends will be no burthen unto me, so that bothe myselfe and
famely may be als hapie in this choyse as in ane higher match.*

This marriage produced the sagacious John Arbuthnott of Fordoun and from
this second family are descended the eighteenth century Viscounts of
Arbuthnott.

Robert, second Viscount was appointed High Sheriff of Kincardineshire in 1658
in the final years of the Protectorate, while still only eighteen. The Roundheads
had hoped to find the Scottish crown jewels hidden in Dunnottar Castle, since
they were in the safekeeping of the Earl Marshal, but they had been smuggled
away to Kinneff Church during the siege. Robert's brother-in-law, Lord Keith,
had escaped to France during the siege of Dunnottar and the authorities had
been duped into thinking he had taken the regalia with him. The second
Viscount, having married into the Keith family, was probably privy to the true
location of the crown jewels and was certainly a witness to their uncovering
from their hiding place after the restoration of the monarchy in 1660.

After Charles II returned to claim his throne, he imposed Episcopalianism
throughout his kingdom. Despite having previously promised to allow
Presbyterianism in Scotland, when he came to power he made Episcopacy the
established Church. It was not in the character of Charles II to be overbearing
and the new era of Episcopacy was gently imposed, services were very similar
to those already taking place, but none the less the organisation was under the
supervision of Bishops.

When Episcopacy was imposed for this second time, Robert, like many other
noblemen and lairds in the North-East, turned his religious allegiance in the
opposite direction to that held so tenaciously by his father. He again held the
patronage of Arbuthnott parish, so could appoint the minister and presented

his relative the Reverend Alexander Arbuthnot as minister in 1665, thereby introducing the second family historian to the living. As part of his personal role in the running of the church, he also presented a list of those candidates deemed suitable as elders. In 1681 he was closely questioned on the conduct of the minister by a visiting inspection team appointed by the Bishop of St Andrews. He took the oath of allegiance, required of all ministers and office holders in the Church, to renounce the Covenant and thereby demonstrate support for the Crown. This was referred to as taking the 'Test' and he took it in Edinburgh in the presence of the President of the Session and others on 24 November 1681:

*Robert, 2nd Viscount, who in his youth was "so inviting" that Lady Elizabeth Keith "fell deeply in love with him at first sight"*

*I own and sincerely profess the true protestant religion contained in the Confession of Faith recorded in the first Parliament of James the sixth. And I farder [further] affirm and swear by this my solemn oath that I judge it unlawful for subjects upon pretence of reformation, or any other pretence whatsoever, to enter into Covenants or Leagues or to convocat, convene or assemble in any Councills, Conventions or Assemblies, and that I shall never rise in arms to enter such Covenants or Assemblies, and that there lyes no obligation in me from the National Covenant or Solemn League and Covenant (so commonlie called), or any manner of way whatsoever to endeavour any change or alteration in the Government, either in Church or State as it is now established by the laws of this Kingdom.*

Laird Robert took this oath against a background of armed opposition to the Government by the Covenanters who had become an extreme, and by now persecuted, minority. Armed rebellion was a strong possibility at that time and the second Viscount played his role as Captain of a militia troop that was held in readiness for such an event. In 1676 he was ordered to take his men to a muster on 3 June at the Bridge of Dee, Aberdeen.

Robert, the second Viscount died on 15 June 1682, the year after he took the Test. He was aged forty-two. Successive generations dubbed him "the Wise Lord" on account of his prudence. He did much to redress the balance of the family's allegiances by supporting the Episcopalian cause. The pendulum of religious opinion was to swing back and forward several more times with successive Lairds.

### Robert, third Viscount and twentieth Laird
### 1682-1694

The third Viscount was twenty-one when he inherited from his father. There was an air of optimism generated by the reign of Charles II, who was a far more astute man than his father and one who recognised that compromise was not a sign of weakness. During his reign tensions relaxed and the arts flourished.

*The drawing room at Arbuthnott House graced by Robert, 3rd Viscount's ornate plaster ceiling, a rare survival of seventeenth century sophistication and skilled craftsmanship.*

On 3 May 1683 the young Laird married the daughter of the Earl of Sutherland, Lady Anne Gordon, who, according to local commentator John Napier in the

*Fraser Papers,* was *"of huge stature".* He then set about improving the house, making it a fit abode for a nobleman and his aristocratic wife, daughter of one of the largest landowners in Scotland. A new entrance was made up a wide stone staircase within the walls of the old castle, where previously only an easily defended circular staircase would have been considered safe. The magnificent plaster ceilings, particularly in the drawing rooms but also in the main bedrooms were made, employing the highest standard of craftsmanship by a master plasterer, probably Robert White, who also worked at Fyvie Castle. Next the spectacular gardens were laid out on the south facing slopes below the house. Walls were built round it and a garden house built in the far north corner. This indicated that life was changing. It was no longer a mere struggle to survive where home was just a refuge, now there was peace, leisure and the time to appreciate beauty. It is sad that the third Viscount and his wife both died in their early thirties and, having had eleven children, only seven survived infancy. The heir, another Robert, was baptised on 24 November 1686.

*Robert, 3rd Viscount, who changed the fortified castle of his ancestors into a graceful manor with a wide stone stair, elegant formal gardens and stylish reception rooms with fancy ceilings.*

The young couple had to cope not only with their big family and embellishments to the house and garden, but also with the difficulties imposed by religious controversy in the outside world. The death of the King led to another period of instability and uncertainty. While Charles II quite possibly remained quietly a Catholic by conviction, he nevertheless had the sense to embrace publicly the Protestant faith, albeit in the form of Episcopalianism. However his brother King James VII (and II of England), was as obdurate as his father Charles I, and was determined to remain a Catholic. This made him so unpopular that after three years, when his wife gave birth to a male heir destined to be raised a Catholic, he was forced to abdicate and flee the country. With this 'Glorious Revolution' of 1688, the throne went to his daughter Mary and her

Protestant husband Prince William of Orange. Since then the Constitution has ordained that no Catholic can inherit the British throne.

In this affair the third Viscount came out firmly on the side of his Kirk Session and the re-establishment of Presbyterianism. His father had been an Episcopalian but he reverted to his grandfather's persuasion. The fifth Viscount was to swing his allegiance back the other way. In the spring of 1689, he went to Edinburgh. On 11 April, at a Scottish convention he signed the Claim of Right, the document drawn up to endorse the claim of William and Mary to the throne. It cited the offences of James VII, forbade another Catholic to be the monarch, and curtailed the previously autocratic powers of the Crown. Not everyone supported the ousting of King James. Graham of Claverhouse, Lord Dundee, left the convention to gather an army of support for the Jacobite cause in the Highlands. This army met King William's supporters at the Battle of Killiecrankie. The Highlanders were victorious but Claverhouse was killed. The Highlanders were held up by a small force at Dunkeld and eventually, leaderless, dispersed into the highlands.

Among the Arbuthnott Family Papers the book of accounts for June 1689 of Robert, third Viscount has the following entry, which shows that he had paid a man to report on the activities of the Highlanders. There must have been a fear that the "*Highland men*" would return to Arbuthnott, some still living would remember the destruction wrought at their last visit in 1644:

> 1. "*To Robt. Forrett for intellegence of Highland men*" 0 14
> (*14 shillings*)

The same list of accounts reads:

> 2. "*Of instrument money taken against the parson upon his refusal to move.*" 0 19 0 (*19 shillings*).

The "*parson*" referred to was the family chronicler, the Reverend Alexander Arbuthnot, still incumbent minister of Arbuthnott, who came out badly over the change in church rule because he was an ardent Jacobite, or supporter of James VII and II. He was willing to sacrifice his position for his convictions. In September 1689, he refused to read from his pulpit the Declaration of Estates which stated that James VII and II had forfeited his crown and that it was offered to William and Mary on condition that Episcopacy in Scotland was to be abolished. He was therefore dismissed from his appointment as minister by order of the Privy Council.

Again religious controversy caused a great deal of bitterness. This was exemplified by the ousting of the Reverend Alexander, as the minutes of the Kirk Session reveal.

> *24th December 1690. Thomas Allardes and James Spark, two of those who were commissioned by the Session to goe to the late*

*incumbent, reported that they went and spoke with him, and
that he refused absolutely to give up the books or bonds or
writts belonging to the Kirk Session till he received payment
from the Viscount of Arbuthnott of the soum of six pounds thirteen shillings and four pennies Scots, for keeping of the library
yearly during his abode in that place. Secondly he claims right
to that desk he formerly possessed by alleging it to have been
given to him by the late Viscount of Arbuthnott. Thirdly he
claims the right to the trees which he planted in the minister's
garden. Also he refused to give up the Session book unfilled up,
neither will he fill it up unless the Session will hire ane clerk
and send him to write it. Whereupon the Session determined to
summon him before the sheriff court against the first January
next.*

The Reverend Alexander retired to Hallgreen, a small estate near Inverbervie
that had recently passed out of the possession of the Arbuthnott family. (It was
granted to Robert, twelfth laird of Arbuthnott in 1487.) He died there in 1691.
After his death, his eldest son John was drawn into the dispute, because
although the books, bonds, writs and other things belonging to the library and
Kirk Session had been restored, he had still refused to hand over the Session
Book.

*8th April 1691. The qlk [which] day it was reported that Mr.
John Arbuthnott, son of the late Alexander Arbuthnott, had now
given up the Session book with the Scrolls thereof to David Raitt,
servitor to the Viscount of Arbuthnott, and that upon reception
of the said book and scrolls the said David Raitt engaged himself to procure a receipt from the Session to the foresaid Mr.
John, but in regard that there had been nothing written in that
book since August 1681, and that the scrolls for the space of six
years are nothing but a rapsidie of confusion, defective, and
wanting in many places of years and months, it is therefore
thought fitt that the Minister, Thomas Allardes and Robert
Arbuthnott meet here on Monday next in order to revising of
the foresaid defects in the Scrolls, and consider the nature and
frame of the said receipt, which accordingly they did.*

The dispute was not yet over, on that same day the entry reads:

*8th April 1691. The qlk day the Viscount Arbuthnott informed
the Session that Mr John Arbuthnott had spoke to him, and
desired to have the liberty of erecting ane tombstone or monument above the grave of his deceased father, Mr. Alexander
Arbuthnott, late incumbent of this congregation, to which the
said Viscount replied it could neither be done without the consent of the heritors, nor without the advice and consent of the
Session, neither without ane bill to the Session desiring the same*

*as is formal in all judiciaries, as also the inscription on the said*
*tombstone must be seen and known, that there may be nothing*
*found therin which may be derogatory to the present*
*Government or reflecting on the present minister at the place.*

Not surprisingly, young Mr John Arbuthnot and his brothers all left Scotland. John went to London, where he became physician to Queen Anne, friend of Pope and Swift and the author of *The History of John Bull*. His brother Robert, who had fought on the Stuart side at the Battle of Killiecrankie, went to Rouen in France, where he started up a bank called 'Arbuthnot et Cie'. Later he moved to Paris where he helped many an exiled Jacobite. Alexander went to India and the youngest, George became a member of Queen Anne's Guard. After her death he also went to France[*].

In 1694 the third Viscount died aged thirty-three, a tragically early death for one with such energy and imagination. There are two portraits of him, one at Arbuthnott House, the other at Crathes Castle, the home of his sister Margaret who married Sir Thomas Burnett of Leys in 1677 and had twenty-one children. He left behind him, not only the portraits, but the exquisite plaster ceilings to remind subsequent generations of the family of what might have been had this cultured man lived longer. His death ushered in a period of unhappy controversy within the family.

### The Minority of the fourth Viscount

On the Viscount's death a family dispute broke out over the management of the estate and guardianship of the children. The third Viscount named his uncle as Tutor to his children in his will, another guardian was to be his brother-in-law, Sir Thomas Burnett. His uncle was Alexander Arbuthnott of Knox, half-brother to the second Viscount and Member of Parliament for Kincardineshire from 1689-1702. Against them were ranged Lady Arbuthnott and her father the Earl of Sutherland. The episode is recorded in *The Scots Peerage*:

> *On Lord Arbuthnott's death his widow, who seems to have dis-*
> *approved of the guardians whom he had appointed to their chil-*
> *dren, including his uncle, Alexander Arbuthnott of Knox, and*
> *his brother-in-law, Sir Thomas Burnett of Leys, succeeded in get-*
> *ting his will set aside on the ground that though a considerable*
> *period had elapsed from the date when he had given instruc-*
> *tions for its preparation, the document was not read over to*
> *him before he signed it.*

The dispute must have been bitter, Robert Chambers' *Domestic Annals of Scotland* records that Lady Arbuthnott petitioned the Privy Council for money and the right to remain at Arbuthnott House. She, being the daughter of an earl, expected a high standard of living with many servants to attend her

---

[*] See Appendix 6 for a brief description of the descendants of the Reverend Alexander

*Lady Anne Gordon, wife of
the 3rd Viscount of
Arbuthnott; her high crown
of curls suggests she was
proud enough of her "huge
stature" to emphasis it. Of
her 11 children, 7 survived
but she died in her early
thirties in 1695.*

children, an extravagance which the appointed guardians may well have considered excessive and which may have been one of the factors in the dispute.
Her petition was to the Scottish Privy Council which was to be abolished in
1708, the year after the Act of Union, when the English and Scottish govern-
ments were combined.

*Provision was made by the Privy Council in March 1695 for the
widowed Viscountess of Arbuthnot (Anne, daughter of the fourteenth Earl of Sutherland), who had been left with seven children all under age, and whose husband's testament had been
'reduced'. In her petition the Viscountess represented that the
estate was twenty four thousand merks per annum (£1,333 ster-
ling). 'My Lord, being now eight years of age, has a governor
and a servant; her two eldest daughters, the one being eleven,
and the other being ten years of age, and capable of all manner
of schooling, they must have at least one servant, as for the
youngest son and the three youngest daughters, they are yet
within the age of seven, so each of them must have a woman to
wait upon them.' Lady Arbuthnot was provided with a jointure
[widow's provision] of twenty-five chalders of victual, and as her
jointure-house [dower-house] was ruinous, she desired leave to
occupy the family mansion of Arbuthnot House, which her son
was not himself of an age to possess. The Lords, having
enquired into and considered the relative circumstances,
ordained that £2,000 Scots (£166 13s. 4d.) should be paid to*

*Lady Arbuthnot out of the estate, for the maintenance of her children, including the young Lord. The Lady soon after dying, the Earl her father came in her place as keeper of the children at the same allowance.*

Lady Arbuthnott died within a year of her husband, the minutes of the Kirk Session read:

*23 June 1695. The qlk day there was no sermon in regard the Minister was obliged to attend Viscountess of Arbuthnott who was departing this life.*

Alexander of Knox had moved swiftly, a record in the Arbuthnott family papers notes:

*17 June 1695. Service of tutoring in favour of Alex. Arbuthnott of Knox, as Tutor to the Viscount of Arbuthnot, Mr John, Lady Jean, Ann, Mary, Margaret and Helen.*

The Earl of Sutherland was not to be bettered so easily. The account in the *The Scots Peerage* suggests that there may have been some justification in his objections to Alexander of Knox as Tutor. Although the Earl's petition against him was not upheld, the Tutor's relatives seem to have left themselves open to court action in guaranteeing his good management of the estates:

*Alexander Arbuthnott [of Knox] then procured himself to be served tutor-at-law to the children as their nearest agnate, whereupon their grandfather, the Earl of Sutherland, presented a petition to Parliament making serious charges against the past admininstration of the estate by the Laird of Knox and Sir Thomas Burnett, and the fitness of the former to be tutor-at-law. Parliament however, on 22 September 1696, wisely remitted the whole matter to the Lords of Session to cognosce and determine therein. It does not appear that Lord Sutherland's charges were held to be established, and the Tutor seems to have had the support of at least two members of the family viz. John Arbuthnott of Fordoun, and Robert Arbuthnott, Provost of Montrose, who, with others, joined in a cautionary obligation for the faithful discharge of his duties. They had, however, to take somewhat stringent measures later on to protect themselves against claims emerging in consequence of the manner in which he administered his ward's estate.*

This dispute gives us interesting evidence of the assets and income of the estate. It is probable that the estate was at its wealthiest in the sixteenth and seventeenth centuries and from now on the relative fortunes of the family were to decline. The Lairds had always provided gifts for the church, but the Arbuthnott family were more generous at this point in the seventeenth century than at any time since Robert, twelfth Laird. They gave four silver communion cups to the kirk, the last two being cast from one larger one left to the church by the third Viscount. A Session minute of 8 March 1696 reads:

> *the qlk* [which] *day the minister informed the session that for as much as the late deceased Viscount Arbuthnott had freely gifted to the Church a silver cup of different form from the rest, and also more than equal weight with the other two, it was therefore deemed good that it were sent to Aberdeen, and cast into two, that so they might have four all of one fashion, form and size, and the Session should pay the goldsmith, to which they all willingly condescended as a good overture, and appointed William Tod, Church Officer, to carry it to Aberdeen with him.*

The fourth Viscount and twenty-first Laird had a sad inheritance. By the time he was nine both his parents were dead. He had experienced much bereavement, two younger brothers and two sisters having also died. His domestic troubles reflected conditions in the country as a whole.

# Chapter 7

## The Ill Years

Throughout the minority of Robert, fourth Viscount, while his grandfather and great-uncle were having their acrimonious dispute over his guardianship and the management of his estate, Scotland was in the grip of an appalling period of bad weather and the resulting bad harvests, *King William's Ill Years* being the name that contemporaries gave this period. There was widespread famine and Arbuthnott parish suffered an influx of starving beggars. They had enough problems caring for their own poor without more refugees. Two extracts from the parish records show the straits that people had come to:

> *22 March 1696. The qlk day the Minister was appoyted to inti-*
> *mate a day for humiliating and fasting to be obsyrved in the*
> *congregation on Wednesday nixt for supplicating Almightie*
> *God that he might turn away from the fierceness of his wrath*
> *which was threatening famine both to man and beast through*
> *the intemperancy, coldness and indisposition of the weather att*
> *this tyme of the year.*

> *5 July 1696. The qlk day the starving conditione of some of the*
> *poor being considered James Allardes was appoynted to give*
> *them the remainder of the bear and meall receaved from my*
> *Lord (Arbuthnott) his mortificatioun* [gift] *either in bear or*
> *meall as he should judge att most convenient.*

The whole of Scotland was affected by the crisis, it was estimated at the time that a fifth of the population were driven to leave their homes and beg for food. Scenes such as are seen in parts of drought-ridden or war-torn Africa today, must have been familiar.

The Arbuthnott parish record gives an insight into the condition of the inhabitants and some ingenious ways of raising revenues to feed the poor. When nearly the entire community in the parish went regularly to the kirk and the population was much larger, there was a considerable problem with space. Lofts or galleries were built to increase the seating capacity and there was a practice of renting these seats on a yearly basis. There was great advantage in sitting upstairs because the ground floor was earthen, the roof leaked and large pools of water collected inside in the wet weather. The collection of these rents was obviously extremely haphazard; this had not been important until the crisis of these years of starvation. Now there was great difficulty in getting the money. People who were happy to forget that they owed money in good times were unlikely to want to pay up when times were bad. From the outset seat rents were a constant trouble to the Session. The new lofts were erected out of the Poor's Fund, and were meant to provide, not only additional accommodation but also a due revenue for the Fund through seat rents. It was in the interests of the Poor that the Session took a stern attitude towards the defaulters. Some were brought before Viscount Arbuthnott's Court, and others were even threatened with legal action.

> *June 19th 1698. The qlk day Mr. William Wright, thesaurer, reported that forasmuch as those who sit in the new Loft had been for some years bygone defective in their payment for seats by which the poor's interest was wronged and notwithstanding that payment had been frequently required yet still they delayed, which being considered they appoyted him to cause summon them before the Viscount of Arbuthnott his court, and obtain decreits against them, and if they would not pay he might cause poynd* (fine) *them.*

So it was that at this time the Viscount Arbuthnott's court is mentioned. Personal courts were still in operation in the lowlands but their powers were reduced by now to dealing with local minor misdemeanors. Any punishment was limited to the imposition of fines. While the Laird was still a minor, the court was presided over by his Tutor in his stead.

By 1706, the year after his Tutor had died, the Laird was eighteen and was drawn personally into the case of the *"scandalous vagabond"*:

> *14 July 1706. The Minister informs the Session that he hears of a scandalous vagabond that gives herself out sometimes under the name of Catanach sometimes under the name of Lindsay who haunts frequently the paroch to the great dishonour of God and the hazard of ensnaring others. The Session taking this to their consideration appoynt William Greig and John Robertson to discharge the Taverners in Boghall to gaive her any entertainment for the future with certification if they doe they will be proceeded against as encouragers of scandal and scandalous persons: appoynts also likewise Francis Molyson to deal with My Lord Arbuthnott's chamberlain to interpose his autie* (authority) *for causing banishing her from his paroch: and the Minister to speake to the Viscount Himself with his first conveninece to the same effect and on the next Lord's day he publickly for the pulpit discharge the whole paroch from conversing with her and giving her entertainment whatsomever.*

In 1707 the English and Scottish Parliaments were united in the Act of Union one hundred years after the Union of the Crowns. In the days before popular opinion had a voice, the pragmatic view prevailed, which was that the alternative would have spelt virtual economic ruin for the Scots. Scotland did however retain her separate legal system and her independent established Church with its governing body, the General Assembly. For the nobility the magnet of the bright lights of London had been a draw since James VI went south to claim his throne. Now all power lay there. Sixteen peers were to be elected to represent their fellows in the House of Lords.

*Robert, fourth Viscount and twenty-first Laird*
*1694-1710*

In 1708, the year following the Act of Union, the young Laird left Arbuthnott for the Grand Tour, the journey round Europe that young nobleman of the eighteenth century undertook to complete their education. He was never to return.

> *Soon after reaching majority, Lord Arbuthnott left Scotland in*
> *1708, appeared with an equipage suiting his quality at the*
> *Court of England, made a campaign in Flanders, travelled*
> *through the Provinces and part of Germany, and returned to*
> *London* [*].

On his return to London he became seriously ill, he had probably contracted tuberculosis. After he had recovered his strength slightly, he wrote a poignant letter home to his cousin:

> *London, 21 March 1710*
> *Sir, - My longe and severe indisposition hath forced me contrair*
> *to my intention to faill in writing to my friends and I must*
> *owne I am wanting that way to you as weell as others; But*
> *now that I begin to take up a little my friends come fresh to my*
> *remembrance so that I cannot longer omitt to inquire of your*
> *health which would be very agreable to me to have confirmed*
> *under your own hand with the remarkable occurances in our*
> *shire. I longe mightily to be att home to see all my good friends*
> *especialy yourselfe whose friendship and good neighbourhood*
> *shall never miss ane just esteem from, Sir, your affectionate*
> *Cousine and very humble servant,*
>
> > *Arbuthnott*

He went to Bath, then just emerging as a fashionable society spa town, in the hope of an improvement but died there in 1710 at the age of twenty-four, only months after this homesick letter was written. His was another brief life, full of unfulfilled promise. He was buried in Bath Abbey, one of the few Lairds not to be buried at Arbuthnott.

---

* From The Scots Peerage, ed. Sir J B Paul

## John, fifth Viscount and twenty-second Laird
## 1710-1756 "the Religious Lord"

When the young fourth Viscount died in 1710, he ended an era of six Roberts; with the inheritance of his younger brother as fifth Viscount, we come to a succession of six Johns.

*"Lord John who succeeded his elder brother Robert and who died in 1756 was the biggest man J N* [John Napier] *ever saw."* This description of the Laird from the *Fraser Papers* tells us that he had inherited his mother's physical stature. The portrait of the fifth Viscount was painted when he was twenty-two on the occasion of his marriage to Jean Morrison, whose picture makes a pair. She was painted in her bright silk gown, he in his peer's robes of scarlet velvet wearing a grey wig which makes him appear older than he was, though the youthful slimness of his figure betrays his age. They both look confident and cheerful, but the marriage had not been approved by William Morrison of Prestongrange, the bride's father, nor indeed by members of the Arbuthnott family. The marriage may have started as a love match, but in later years it had its stormy passages if the evidence of the *Fraser Papers* is to be believed:

> *The Religious Lord had several differences with his Lady, the last of which occasioned him to separate and live in a separate wing of the house. It happened that his Lordship in conversing with some of his visitors on religious topics often quoted the Apostle Paul, when her Ladyship exclaimed "Pox on you and the Apostle Paul too. You pay more respect to him than Lady Arbuthnott." On which his Lordship ordered her out of the room. After his death she spoke of him with respect and regretted she had not bridled her passion observing that "if any person get to Heaven he certainly will".*

Even in the early days of their marriage, there were already signs of the young man's profligacy and his headstrong nature. A description in *The Scots Peerage* tells of his youthful extravagance:

> *His Lordship's administration of his affairs, at all events at the outset, does not appear to have been characterised by frugality, and the estate of Arrat had to be sold.*

and the *Fraser Papers* have this verdict:

> *His Lordship was a man of strict honour and very religious, but not otherwise possessed of great mental endowments.*

This was a dangerous mix for the times in which he lived because John, fifth Viscount had an abiding passion, that of the Jacobite cause. Arrat, the estate bought from the Erskines of Dun in 1591, may well have had to be sold to provide the £20,000 that he gave to his factor, Robert Thomson, in 1715 to fund the doomed cause of the first Jacobite rebellion.

The Jacobites were supporters of the Stuart line and deplored the 'Glorious Revolution'. However, while William and Mary, and then Queen Anne, sister of Mary and younger daughter of James VII remained on the throne, the Jacobites could tolerate the situation. Sadly, although Anne bore seventeen children, she died in 1714 without an heir and the throne went to her cousin the Elector of Hanover. The passing of the British monarchy from the House of Stuart to the House of Hanover was too much for the Jacobites to bear and plots were laid immediately for the restoration of the Stuarts. The contender for the throne was the 'Old Pretender' or King James VIII as his supporters called him, whose birth had precipitated the ousting of his father James VII (and II). He came to Scotland in 1715 in a lacklustre effort to regain the throne. Later, in 1745, his elder son the 'Young Pretender' or 'Bonnie Prince Charlie' as he was popularly known, personally led the second Jacobite rebellion. Many Scots, particularly Highlanders, suffered banishment, forfeiture of title and property and even death in support of these two men. The tragedy was that both pretenders possessed the worst of the Stuart characteristics. Although undoubtedly brave, they were indecisive and had a total inability to grasp the reality of a situation. However their royal charisma and their Catholicism made them the embodiment of a romantic dream; the restoration of the Stuart monarchy and with it the colourful and ritualistic High Church.

An informer wrote of plans for the first rebellion in 13 August 1715:

> *We hear from Strathbogie that the Marquis of Huntly has been taken up with preparations this summer, specially in buying horses and using them to the Drum. He is said to have 600 of them scattered up and down the country well equipped and a great number of foot as well appointed. He has employed one Peter McKoul, an old trooper, to list men for the Pretender. From Angus and Mearns we hear that the Earl Marischal is fitting up Dunottar for a garrison, and is already said to have a good Magazine of arms and Ammunition. Also that he has bought up and dyed great parcels of cloth for soldiers clothes. This is reported by those who sold cloth and spoke to the man who dyed it. That the Earl Marischal, Viscount Arbuthnot and other have frequent meetings in the night time at the Earl of Southesk's house, that the like meetings are kept at the laird of Powry's house, where also Ogilvie of Boyn is said to be, against whom this was a proclamation emitted in 1708 \**.

In 1715 the Old Pretender landed in Scotland, but, after an ineffective campaign, the Jacobites lost the Battle of Sheriffmuir against the Government forces under the Duke of Argyll. A contemporary remarked that the Old Pretender, by his indecisiveness in arriving after the battle was over, waiting around after-

---

* Quoted by George Henderson in The Kirk of St Ternan, Arbuthnott

wards and burning two villages for which he left money as compensation, showed that he was "*of the family*". He then left for France by ship from Montrose.

Among the nineteen peers who lost their titles was the Earl Marshal. He had taken such a prominent part in the 1715 rising that he forfeited not only his title, but his offices and his home, Dunnottar Castle, which was then turned into a ruin, by the removal of the roofs and floors. He spent the rest of his life in exile. The Viscount's uncle, John Arbuthnott of Fordoun, was chosen to replace the Earl Marshal as Sheriff of Kincardine. Among the Arbuthnott family papers is the following document:

> *Commission by George I to John Arbuthnot of Fordoun being that the office of Sheriff Principal of the county of Kincardine has been vacant and in the King's hands by reason of the forfeiture of the Earl Marischal and the King being fully satisfied of the faith and integrity of the aforesaid Arbuthnot of Fordoun and of his qualifications for the said office, and therefore nominating and appointing him to the Office of Sheriff Principal of the said County during his pleasure with all the privileges pertaining thereto whatsoever*
>
> *6 June 1716.*

The Laird's involvement in the 1715 rising was not confined to a large donation of £20,000. We have evidence from the diarist, John Napier, quoted in the *Fraser Papers*, that he also sent men to fight in the abortive Battle of Sherriffmuir:

> *Lord John having been a stiff Jacobite sent out a company of men to join King James at Sheriffmuir but his factor a Robert Thomson having taken blame on himself the Estate was secured from forfeiture.*

Certain circumstances allowed the fifth Viscount to remain at Arbuthnott at that point. The first was, as John Napier tells us, the loyalty of his factor who took the blame for his own involvement. Secondly, he did not personally take up arms and thirdly, his uncle John Arbuthnott of Fordoun was appointed the Sheriff of Kincardineshire. His close relations did not share his enthusiasm for the Stuarts. They were content with the government of the day.

John the fifth Viscount was known as the 'Religious Lord', and it was his strongly felt high church leanings, (directly opposite to those held by his father the third Viscount) which spurred on his adherence to the Jacobite cause. In 1715 he built an Episcopalian chapel at Boghall for those who, like himself, did not wish to worship at the kirk, where since 1688, after the ousting of Alexander Arbuthnot, the services had been Presbyterian. By then Presbyterianism was the established Scottish Church, and indeed was to remain so until the present day. Presbyterian services are still conducted in the kirk.

In 1732 the old wooden bridge over the Bervie near the kirk was in such a constant state of disrepair that plans were made to replace it with a stone bridge in order to allow those people living on the south side of the river to be able to attend the kirk. As recorded in the Session minutes the minister showed the plans for the bridge "*to the Viscount of Arbuthnott who much relished the design and promised to furnish the whole lime for the said bridge and also to give all the timber growing near the Bridge and in James Lindsey's yard to help defray the Charges*".

*Charles Edward Stuart, 'Bonnie Prince Charlie' who, however bonny he may have been, led the Scots to a disastrous defeat at Culloden in 1746 and nearly cost that enthusiastic Jacobite, John, 5th Viscount his title and estate.*

By 1745 the laird's preoccupation was again with the Jacobite cause. That year Prince Charles, the Young Pretender, arrived in Scotland and set up his standard at Glenfinnan. If he expected whole-hearted support, he did not get it. The Scots were divided; as with any civil war, even families were divided. Most of his supporters were Highlanders. Gradually the Prince collected a sizeable army and its progress gathered momentum. This rising was a far more serious affair than the previous one. The army reached Edinburgh and the Prince was installed at Holyrood where he held daily councils "*and according to Lord George Murray in a letter to his brother it comprised the Duke of Atholl as President, Earl Wemyss, Lords Strathallan, Arbuthnott*". The factor Robert Thomson was again involved and made the tenants at Arbuthnott contribute levy money for the rebels. He tried to join the rebel army in Edinburgh "*but for his waiting upon the Young Pretender and not getting a station from him suitable to his ambition, he returned home and has lived quietly ever since".*

A kindly but indiscreet letter survives which shows the tragedy of civil war and how it affected the lives of individuals. It was written by the fifth Viscount to an officer in the Prince's Army on behalf of Lady Nicolson of Glenbervie, whose beloved pony had been commandeered for the rebel army's use.

> *To Colonel James Moir of Stonywood*
> *In the Princes Camp*
>
> *Sir*
> *I have putt the enclosed under this cover, which you'l please take the trouble to deliver to Lord Pitsligo with your conveniency. Lady Nicolson has not recovered her own sadle horse which was a blue pownie and can be of little use for camp. I am hopefull you'l be able to prevail with Captain M'Innes and Birkenbuss, to return him, which will do the Lady a singular favour, as it will not be an easy matter for her to find out any other horse that pleases her so well as this does. The bearer gave me a very particular and distinct account of the late battle near Falkirk in which the Prince's army gained a complete victory, and without very great loss on their side, which was a very extraordinary thing considering the regular army they had to contend with and the experienced generals that commanded it: but God has all along in a very surprizing manner favoured the Prince's cause and I am hopeful he will ever continue to do so to the end. The town of Aberdeen is in the greatest confusion and disorder imaginable; and if something is not done soon to preserve peace and order in it, it is much to be feared that the inhabitants will enter into blood with each other, which I wish may be prevented in time. God Almighty preserve you from all the dangers you should be exposed to in the field and every where else, and keep you alwaies under His special care and providence. I offer my compliments to your uncle and all friends, and am, Sir*
>
> *Your most humble Servant*
>
> *Arbuthnott*
>
> *Arbuthnot January 31st 1745/6.*

# Chapter 8

## Culloden and After

The Prince's cause however was doomed. His army initially swept down into England and looked likely to reach London. Through indecision, the impetus was never maintained and the Government army under the Duke of Cumberland, son of King George II, had time to organise and slowly pushed the Jacobites back. Finally, on 16 April 1746, the two armies met at Culloden, near Inverness. The Jacobite defeat was absolute. The Prince wandered in the highlands for five months with a thirty thousand pound price on his head, until he was finally rescued off the west coast by a French ship.

Retribution against the rebels was terrible. The Duke earned the name 'Butcher Cumberland'. Culloden was a massacre, and of those who were not killed then, many were executed, some died in prison and some were transported. The Highlanders had been most involved and they suffered most. There, where the old way of life under their chieftains had remained unchanged, the effect of the defeat was devastating. A series of statutory restrictions were introduced aimed particularly at the highland way of life including the abolition of private jurisdiction, since in the highlands the Clan Chiefs' hereditary judicial courts had retained their powers while in the lowlands the power of the similar barons' courts had been gradually weakened. In addition, the wearing of tartan and the bearing of arms were outlawed. The effect of these draconian measures was profound. However those who lived in any part of Scotland and had been involved risked at the most death, at the least confiscation of property. In the case of John, 5th Viscount of Arbuthnott the danger was averted, but not without a large element of good fortune.

After the Battle of Sheriffmuir in 1715, when the Old Pretender's forces were defeated, he hid certain incriminating documents in his chapel. After Culloden, however, he was advised by John Young the Sheriff Clerk of the county to take these papers out and burn them. This friendly gesture shows how he escaped prosecution to some extent due to the affection in which he was held. Another example of this is shown by an incident involving a tenant of one of his most prosperous farms. This man went to Sheriff Young with incriminating evidence against his Laird. He was told he could have his farm as his own if he could find another tenant who would be similarly rewarded to support his testimony. This the man failed to do, the other tenants all remaining loyal, perhaps out of affection for their dangerously single-minded Laird and because they also had sympathy for the Jacobite cause.

The attitude of Sheriff Young and the Arbuthnott tenants gives a clue to one major reason why the fifth Viscount, while so deeply involved in the 'Forty-five', still managed to escape punishment. Another likely reason lay in the fact that the Viscount and his wife were childless. His heir was his cousin John, son of John Arbuthnott of Fordoun, the man who took over as Sheriff Principal of Kincardine after the Earl Marshal had forfeited that position in 1715. The heir to the estates was therefore the son of a trusted Government supporter.

However, there is no doubt that the Viscount felt vulnerable enough to take drastic action. In addition to his papers at the Episcopalian chapel, he had to destroy all other family papers, except those strictly concerned with deeds of property. John Duncan, who became an agent to the family and was privy to the family accounts, estimated that the *"Jacobean adventures"* had cost the family £60,000. The Laird did, however, suffer some harassment. In August 1746, the unhappy old man wrote a letter of complaint against the officer in charge of the garrison at Inverbervie complaining at the forfeiture of his arms:

*Viscount Arbuthnott to the Earl of Albemarle*

*My Lord,*
*Tho I have not the good fortune of your aquaintance, yet am I*
*under a necessity to give your Lordship the trouble of this letter*
*in order to lay before you a late act of injustice committed*
*against me by Lieutenant Draper and his Dragoons of*
*Cobhams Regiment now lying at Bervie, and at the same time*
*to demand such reparation and redress as my case requires:*
*how soon my Lord Acrams order for delivering up the Arms of*
*Rebels and other was published, I aquainted Mr Draper by let-*
*ter what Arms I was Master of, and which were no more than*
*what I am privileged to have by law, viz a silver handed sword,*
*two mourning ones, two pair of pistols for my own use and my*
*servants, and a fouling piece for my own diversion which I go*
*to sport. I should have thought that Mr Draper woud not have*
*adventured so far as to take these Arms from me, which are so*
*necessary for me to have, but he has done it in the most*
*arbitary and forcible manner imaginable; for on Munday last*
*he sent up a party of Dragoons here under a Sergeant, who had*
*orders to demand from me in his name the delivery of these*
*Arms mentioned in my letter to him, and with all assuring me*
*that if I did not comply, that the party he had sent would either*
*burn my house, or committ such other outrages as it should*
*think proper,so I was obliged to deliver up all these Arms, and*
*none now of any kind whatsoever either for my own proper use*
*or for my servants when they travel with me abroad; as this is a*
*very hard case, so I am persuaded your Lordship will grant me*
*such satisfaction as I have good title to demand, both as a Peer*
*and a subject that has alwies lived peaceably and quietly under*
*the government, and never done any one thing to provoke this*

*displeasure. I must moreover plead that your LoPs would grant me a protection to peace or tranquility, when I have an Officer in my neighbourhood who is ever molesting and disturbing me all that lyes in his power, and creating me all the trouble and uneasyness imaginable.*

*I expect from your LoPs Justice, honour and fair character that you will grant a favourable return to this my letter, which will be most acceptable and obliging to him, who is with all respect my Lord,*
   *Yours LoPs most Obedient and most humble servant*

    *Arbuthnott*

 *Arbuthnott House, August 3th 1746*

Again the following year he wrote to the Reverend Robert Forbes, pleading the case of a prisoner at Carlisle under sentence of death. However even his family may have felt they must put him under constraint if Arbuthnott was to be saved. That year, 1747, he handed over the running of the estate to his heir, his cousin John.

*Arbuthnott House around 1829 with the Bothenoth to the left. This is the mansion house the 6th Viscount created and it remains almost unaltered to this day.*

From this point until the end of his life, he seems to have lived on while his heir took over not only the estate but, to some extent, his home. He seems to have agreed to making radical changes to the house which must have made it an uncomfortable place to live. These changes involved pulling down the old North Keep and building in its place a wing to match the seventeenth century south wing. The two wings were to be joined by a middle section on the site of the old gatehouse, also three storeys high "*with garret*". The contract with John Ferrior, a builder from Montrose also stipulated that "*the said Viscount obliges himself to furnish all Carriages with Men and Horses and to cause transport all the materials and Implements that shall be wanted to the fore-said building and work from the beginning to the final compleating there-of*". By April 1755 the demolition had been finished and for the next year the building work went on. As Harry Gordon Slade writes:

> *If family tradition is correct the Jacobite 5th Viscount was a builder malgre lui, and must have been cooling in his grave as the builders moved out of the new house, which was due to be completed by Whit Sunday* [mid-May] *1756.*

The fifth Viscount died in May 1756, just before the planned completion of the new house. Perhaps this uncomfortable end to his days was not an unreasonably cruel fate for the Jacobite Laird, when he had cost the family such a vast sum of money and risked the confiscation of the family title and property in his loyalty to the lost cause of the Stuarts. Locally, however, there was genuine grief at his death:

> *J N* [John Napier] *heard the late Mr. Sharp preach his funeral sermon, from the text 'The righteous perish and no man layeth it to heart' etc. calling him 'an Israelite indeed in whom there was no guile.' Many people shed tears and cried aloud on this occasion.*

### John, sixth Viscount and twenty-third Laird
### 1756-1791 "the Rich Lord"

By the time he inherited from his cousin in 1756, John the sixth Viscount had been running the estate for nine years and had been married twice. His first wife, Marjorie Douglas died without children and after her death he married Jean Arbuthnot in 1749. Jean was the daughter of Alexander Arbuthnot of Findowrie, a descendant of Robert, fourteenth Laird of Arbuthnott. Her elder sister Margaret was heiress to the Findowrie estate and married her neighbour, James Carnegy of Balnamoon. Descendants of that family still live at Balnamoon, which, though now far from Arbuthnott lands, was at this time a neighbouring estate. John had three sons and two daughters by Jean.

The sixth Viscount and his wife suffered the premature death of two of these three sons. The heir, Robert, Master of Arbuthnott, died in 1785. His younger brother, Hugh, was already dead, so the title was destined for the third brother, John. Mrs P S-M Arbuthnot's description of the death of Hugh, underlines the continuing perils of travel:

*Hugh, drowned while crossing the Southesk, a little above
Brechin, 2nd October, 1778. John Moir says of him that he
'perished in the Southesk ... coming from Forfar in a chaise,
which was overturned in the river at the ford of Auldbar, by
the carelessness of the driver, who was intoxicated. Mr
Arbuthnott got safe out, but venturing in to attempt the rescue
of the horses, was carried beyond his depth and drowned'.*

John, sixth Viscount worshipped in the kirk. Again the pendulum had swung
and the religious interests of the new Laird were in direct opposition to his predecessor. Where his Jacobite cousin was Episcopalian, the sixth Viscount was a
staunch Presbyterian. We learn of the marriage of their daughter, Margaret
from the Session minutes of the kirk:

*23 April 1768 The reason for this day's Collection made more
than usual was the charity given by Mr Dumbar of Thunderton
and Lord Arbuthnott's daughter attending public worship there
this first Sunday after their marriage.*

On 3 January 1780 Alexander Shank, the minister for thirty-seven years, died.
On 27 June 1780 his son, John, was presented as the new minister by Lord
Arbuthnott after an unusual controversy, as the Session minutes again report:

*1780-1818. John Shank. At the University studied law of
which he tired. For the next eight to ten years studied theology
at home. Never took a divinity course, but the Presbytery finding his knowledge equal, if not superior, to what is expected of
persons who have attended the ordinary curriculum of six
years, recommended him to the Synod for probationary trials.
Synod refused. Presbytery appealed to the General Assembly,
and appeal upheld. Licensed by Presbytery of Fordoun on 27th
June 1780 and presented the same day by John, Viscount of
Arbuthnott. Ordained 20th September the same year. Died
10th December 1818."*

Hard times were to come to Arbuthnott again through bad weather, making the
people's lives a misery and affecting the harvest. The severe winter of 1782 followed a summer of rain and poor harvests. The sixth Viscount is reported giving help to the efforts of the kirk to support the poor, but conditions were so
bad that the Government was forced to produce emergency funds to prevent
the people starving and the Kirk Session tells of a grant to northern Scotland in
which the Arbuthnott parish shared:

*27 June 1783 ... Reverend Sir, The Lords of the Treasury having
directed the Barons of the Exchequer to draw for £10,000, to be
employed in assisting the Poor in the Highlands and Northern
parts of Scotland in this time of scarcity, I am commanded by
their Lordships that you will with all possible dispatch call a*

*meeting of the Heritors and Elders of your Parish, and make up and transmit to me the number of your Poor upon your Poor's Roll, the funds you have or expect to raise for their support, the additional number of poor that you think ought to receive assistance if your funds were larger, and upon the whole what number of bolls of meal will be sufficient, in addition to the funds you have and expect to afford a reasonable support to those who cannot contribute to their own maintenance by their labour, and to those who can only contribute in part, till they can be relieved by the crop of this year.*

*Exchequer Chambers, Edinburgh, signed D.K.R. 21st June, 1783*

Bureaucratic language was no simpler in the eighteenth century than it is today.

The suffering of the poor and the loss of his eldest son in 1785 had its affect on the sixth Viscount, as the family notes in the *The Scots Peerage* recount:

*In his later years he developed considerable eccentricity, which manifested itself in various ways, and in particular with regard to the management of his estates.*

**The Hanoverian 6th Viscount of Arbuthnott, "the Rich Viscount" Ironically it was his eccentricities in old age which earned him this epithet rather than his youthful temperance, taste and sense.**

By the time he died he had left a legacy of farms let at totally uneconomical rents. This was a complication that his heir had to unravel before he could make the improvements that he wished to implement on the estate. Reform was necessary in order to avoid the hitherto inevitable and tragic cycle of bad harvests followed by dearth and starvation.

In spite of being a first cousin of the fifth Viscount, therefore of the same generation, John survived him for thirty-five years, dying in 1791. In his old age, he may have become a difficult old man, but he had achieved a considerable amount for the family during his lifetime. When he inherited, the enormous rebuilding scheme for the house, which he must largely have instigated, had just been completed. It left the family home looking dramatically different from the castle which it replaced and reflected the changed situation in society. Civil war and internal strife were at last to be a thing of the past; the defeat of the Jacobite rebellion ended open warfare in Scotland. The sixth Viscount and his father, John Arbuthnott of Fordoun, had worked for this stability. Both were supporters of the Hanoverians and this was an important reason why the family title and estate were not forfeited despite the escapades of the fifth Viscount. Pragmatism may seem unattractive in comparison to Romanticism, but it can improve the quality of life. This improvement in living standards was to be the hallmark of the times of his son and grandson as Laird.

## The Rebirth of Scotland

After Culloden and the destruction of the old Highland way of life, the pragmatic lowland outlook was given free rein to prevail. During the latter part of the eighteenth century, a remarkably gifted group of Scots were leading the world in various ways. Thomas Telford the civil engineer, Adam Smith the economist and James Watt the inventor of the steam engine, without which the industrial revolution could not have happened, were all Scots. Edinburgh burgeoned with the building of the Georgian New Town and while Robert Adam was not alone in designing this beautiful and imaginative scheme, it was his name which became synonymous with a new architectural style, neo-classicism. In painting and portraiture Raeburn and Ramsay were recognised among the greatest of their day. However, it was in the world of literature that the greatest impact was made on the outlook of Scots themselves, which slowly restored the feeling of identity that they had lost. After the defeat of the Jacobites, sympathy with the idea of 'Scottishness' was unfashionable. This first changed with the emergence of the great national poet Robert Burns, who restored a pride in the Scots tongue and proved that a man of humble origins could rise to prominence, thanks to the inherent Scottish respect for education. This trait has meant that throughout the nineteenth century and beyond, Scotland has exported talent and expertise in medicine, engineering, business management, finance and banking and other disciplines all over the world. It was not a brain-drain, there always was plenty more where it came from, but an enriching of the world at large by a small, multi-talented nation.

The second literary figure to move public opinion towards pride in being

*An engraving of Arbuthnott at the turn of the 19th century with the banks of the Bervie drained and fenced as pasture, the work of the Improving Laird, John, 7th Viscount. In the background Arbuthnott House, with Hugh, 9th Laird's two storey manor house to the rear of the main 17th century block.*

Scottish, rightly has an imposing monument in Princes Street, Edinburgh. It was in the early nineteenth century that Sir Walter Scott made his name with the publication of *The Minstrelsy of the Scottish Border*, an anthology of ballads among which was the legend of Hugh le Blond. He then went on to write his famous series of 'Waverley' novels portraying a vivid and intriguing picture of events in Scottish history. The heroic style of these books kindled an image of the beauty and romance of Scotland in the public imagination. In the summer of 1822 Scott instigated and stage-managed the visit of George IV to Edinburgh, the first monarch since the seventeenth century to visit Scotland. The King, dressed from head to toe in tartan, enjoyed his visit to the full. At a banquet in his honour, such was his pleasure at the evening's entertainment that he told his host, the Lord Provost of Edinburgh, who was William Arbuthnot, a member of the Aberdeenshire branch of the family, that if he managed to walk once round the long dining table without support, instead of the knighthood he was due to receive, he would earn himself a baronetcy. The feat was accomplished and the King kept his word.

### John, seventh Viscount and twenty-fourth Laird
### 1791-1800 "the Improving Laird"

*A great bar to improvement in this parish is the want of roads, there being hardly a track in it which deserves the name.*

This was the verdict given by the author of the first statistical account of the parish of Arbuthnott written in 1794. The lowland landscape had remained unchanged over the centuries, the countryside still consisted of vast stretches of treeless bogland. "*A Tree might be a show in Scotland, as a horse in Venice*" was Doctor Johnson's verdict when he made his journey through Scotland in 1773. Roads were virtually non-existent and methods used to farm the meagre areas of arable land were still primitive. The result was unremitting hardship for the population. Housing conditions were not much better than they had ever been.

When the seventh Viscount inherited from his father, John, sixth Viscount, in 1791, the winds of change in land management were blowing strongly. They were felt particularly by Lord Arbuthnott because he was lucky in having, as near neighbour, a leading exponent of the new farming methods. Robert Barclay of Urie, near Stonehaven, had studied agriculture in Norfolk and, after marrying the heiress to Allardice in the parish of Arbuthnott, he started to carry out improvements to both these estates. He had the waste lands by the river Bervie cleared of stone and after fertilising with lime he introduced a rotation of crops, which included oats, barley, wheat, clover, peas and turnips. He also bound his tenants to long leases to encourage them to keep to this regime. Immediately the quality of stock improved through better feeding stuffs, thus fetching better prices. The yield on the lands improved to such an extent that over twenty years the rents increased to four times their previous value.

Lord Arbuthnott very soon followed Barclay's lead. In 1792 he built the Home Farm steading, the best building of its kind in the neighbourhood, and he also granted long leases of nineteen years to his tenants and insisted on five or seven shift rotations. He also drained the stretches of marshy lands on both banks of the Bervie and built embankments to safeguard this reclamation. He invested in the new farm implements and machinery then becoming available.

The Arbuthnott estate played a pivotal role in the economy of the parish. The 1794 statistical account of the parish gives a surprisingly detailed picture:

> *Heritors etc. - The proprietors are four in number of whom only one is resident, The Viscount of Arbuthnott.*

> *Ecclesiaftical State - With respect to the ecclesiaftical state of the parish: The Viscount of Arbuthnott is patron of the church.*

| | |
|---|---|
| *The number of males is* | *494* |
| *females* | *547* |
| | *1041* |

| | |
|---|---|
| *Of these under 10 years of age, males* | *104* |
| *females* | *147* |
| | *251* |

| | |
|---|---|
| *Bachelors, householders* | *15* |
| *Widows* | *47* |
| *Widowers* | *15* |
| *Gardeners* | *6* |
| *Wrights and house carpenters* | *7* |
| *Masons* | *2* |
| *Taylors* | *5* |
| *Shoemakers* | *8* |
| *Weavers* | *20* |
| *Dyer* | *1* |
| *Millers (at 3 corn mills)* | *4* |
| *Smiths (smith shops being 5)* | *7* |
| *Shopkeepers* | *2* |
| *Wheelwrights* | *2* |
| *Cooper* | *1* |
| *Carrier* | *1* |
| | |
| *There are inhabited houses* | *230* |
| *Of which inhabited by single persons* | *27* |
| *Houses of 2 inhabitants, chiefly old people and newly married* | *35* |
| *Of 3 inhabitants* | *29* |
| *Ale-houses* | *2* |
| *Uninhabited houses (cause, removal of cottagers)* | *6* |

The seventh Viscount made use of the local carpenters and masons to make some imaginative improvements to the house. He added the main staircase lit by a cupola and the portico to the outside entrance. This allowed the family to move for the first time from the bedrooms on one side of the house to the other without going down one stair and up another. The front of the house has not changed since. He planted the beech avenue which leads down to the entrance and gives the upstairs dining room a spectacular view. This was part of a landscaping plan which was carried on by his son.

He married Isabella Grahame and had nine sons and two daughters. His youngest son, Alexander, emigrated to Canada in 1819, with his wife and infant son. This son died unmarried but their four daughters are the forebears of some of the Canadian Arbuthnott family members. John, seventh Viscount died on 27 February 1800 in Edinburgh. By the time of his death, his energy and enthusiasm for progress had brought the family to the point where the nineteenth century seemed to offer only opportunities for further growth and prosperity. His eldest son, John, eighth Viscount stepped into the new century with a modernised and efficient estate and a comfortable and stylish family house.

# Chapter 9

## Victorian Follies

When Queen Victoria came to the throne in 1837, she fell in love with Scotland. She bought the Balmoral estate and spent every summer there. Her example set the fashion and the Scottish highland ideal prevailed, epitomised by the paintings of Sir Edwin Landseer, particularly the picture of a proud stag called *The Monarch of the Glen*. The rich and fashionable bought highland estates and used them for shooting. This was of no benefit to the population at large and encouraged Scottish landowners to think that life was only about the pursuit of leisure activities, without any thought as to how this way of life could be financially sustained other than from the land.

The view held by the Victorian nobility was that only a very limited number of careers were suitable for a gentleman. This meant that few of the old Lairds benefited from the growth in trade, particularly shipping and the manufacturing industries which became so prosperous during the second half of the nineteenth century. This loss of opportunity was matched with a fashion for enlarging country houses. Imitations of Balmoral Castle sprang up. Enormous wings were built on to house the armies of servants which were needed to look after the large house parties of guests, invited to enjoy the amenities of fishing and shooting that were so much in vogue. This left a legacy in the twentieth century of overlarge houses in Scotland which fell into decay through lack of finance. This was first felt when servants disappeared to serve in the First World War. A few returned to their old duties but it was after the Second World War that the impact of social change was such that the upkeep of such houses became an impossibility.

Arbuthnott House was not one of them. Ultimately it was to have been a blessing in disguise that the eighth Viscount was unable to finance additions that he planned for the house in 1839, particularly because these plans had the current trend towards large quarters for the servants in mind. The house therefore remained the manageable size that it is to this day. At the time though it must have been seen as a great disappointment. It was first sign of the disaster which culminated in a family trauma, caused by the disgrace and flight of the eighth Viscount, which seems to have cast a spell of gloom and despondency over Arbuthnott House, which was to last for the next seventy years. This mood culminated in a situation where it was only by a miracle that the house was not either demolished or sold. The period of inactivity and inertia seems to mirror the mood that prevailed in the family after the murder of Sheriff Melville and which lasted much the same length of time, about seventy years.

### John, eighth Viscount and twenty-fifth Laird
### 1800-1860 "the Vanishing Viscount"

The eighth Viscount inherited in 1800, and despite the improved methods of farming, within a few months of his father's death the young Laird was still facing the problem of feeding the poor of the parish.

> *1 June 1800  The Minister informed the Session that the*
> *Viscount of Arbuthnott had ordered ten Bolls of his meal to be*
> *sold at the reduced price of fifteen pence per peck to such people*
> *in the parish that were not able to give more for meal*

By the time the minister, the Reverend James Milne made a second statistical report of the parish in 1843, the population was found to be declining. This was consistent with the general decline in the rural population at that time due to the agricultural revolution which reduced the need for labour.

| *Population changes -* | *1784* | *1811* | *1831* |
|---|---|---|---|
|  | *1841* | *968* | *944* |

To balance this decline, the agricultural revolution had brought increasing prosperity to lowland Scotland. These were times of peace and political stability which encouraged investment. This happened in the case of road building. There had been a significant change in the means of access to Arbuthnott since 1784. By 1838 the Reverend James Milne could write:

> *A great road leading through Stonehaven and Laurencekirk passes*
> *through the northern end of the parish for two miles and a half. An*
> *excellent road has lately been made through the lower part of the*
> *parish extending from the bridge of Bervie which forms the eastern*
> *extremity to the bridge of Whiteriggs, which is the western, a dis-*
> *tance of five miles.*

One aspect of the increase in prosperity since 1784 upset the minister, Mr Milne, "*Inns - There are 5 inns or alehouses; and that number might be reduced with benefit to the morals of the people.*"

The eighth Viscount also made many improvements to the landscape, among others he built a fine classical bridge at Arbuthnott House and he planted trees, as the minister's survey reports: "*Plantations - Most plantations in the parish belong to Viscount Arbuthnott but as they have been formed chiefly by the present proprietor, they are immature. The finest old wood is around the House of Arbuthnott and it is seldom profaned by the axe.*" One plantation was on the lower slopes of Strathfinella Hill, not far from the Cairn o'Mount where the family still held lands.

*John, 8th Viscount's visions of grandeur: the bridge over the Bothenoth built in 1821*

The eighth Viscount married Margaret Ogilvy in 1805. A minor family scandal erupted the same year when his sister Catherine left home to marry the tutor to the younger members of the family, the Reverend David Lyell, who became the minister at Careston. This marriage produced a continued coolness between the Arbuthnott family and the Lyells. David Lyell had private means, however, and he and Catherine spent all their married years at Careston, Catherine making, according to a lady parishioner, "*a capital minister's wife*". After the death of the Dowager Viscountess Isabella in 1818, the eighth Viscount made improvements to the house, adding a decorated plasterwork ceiling to the dining room and changing the fireplaces and windows in the principal rooms. These were the first of extensive plans for building works he conceived.

The eighth Viscount was Lord Lieutenant of Kincardineshire (an office created by the Militia Act of 1797, in response to the fear of an invasion by the French under Napoleon Bonaparte) and representative peer at the House of Lords from 1818-1847. In 1820 he set about getting the family papers in order and engaged the services of a scribe called George Hume from Edinburgh to transcribe many documents and the two family histories. His work in the parish as reported in the Session minutes included arbitrating in local disputes:

> *14 October 1821.*
> *To penalty from John Carcharie*          *16/-Stg.*
> *To penalty from James Robert*          *5/-Stg.*
> *being the fines imposed in consequence of a quarrel between*
> *them agreably to Viscount Arbuthnott's decision to whom the*
> *case was submitted by parties.*

He also supported, as did the sixth Viscount, the local candidate as prospective minister, though again the choice did not go undisputed:

> *1821-50. James Milne M.A. Son of innkeeper at Kirktoun of Arbuthnott. Became Schoolmaster of Arbuthnott. Ordained (assistant and successor) to Garvock 9th May 1814. Presented by John, Viscount of Arbuthnott January 1819, but not translated and admitted till 1st March 1821. Delay caused by a competing presentation in favour of James Miller, preacher of the Gospel. Case came before Presbytery and referred to General Assembly. Finally court of Session rejected Miller's presentation. Wrote the Second Statistical Account of the parish in 1843. Died 24th January 1850.*

There was a tradition that the Kirk Session should possess a mortcloth to adorn the coffin at funerals. Made of velvet with silver trimming, it could be hired out and the money used for the Poor's Fund. On 9 November 1823 "*a new mortcloth was presented to the Kirk Session by the Right Honourable Viscount Arbuthnott value Twelve pounds fourteen shillings per acct of Messrs John Beattie and Co, Montrose*".

The face of the eighth Viscount has become familiar to succeeding generations of his family because a handsome portrait was painted of him by Sir David Wilkie from which prints were made that hang in many of his descendants' houses. Only recently was it discovered that his life ended in tragedy and disgrace. Such disgrace, indeed, that the whole episode was never mentioned in the family and successfully covered up until, in March 1992, an article written by S Scott Robinson appeared in the Journal of the Law Society of Scotland entitled *The Vanishing Viscount* and revealed the whole story.

The tragedy began in 1829 when the Laird had a serious accident, most probably as a result of a fall from a horse. He suffered a severe head injury resulting in brain damage. It is clear by comparing his activities before and after this event, that his character underwent a gradual change. Over the years his behaviour became more and more erratic until, exacerbated by financial problems, it led him to break the law.

Costly improvements to the estate and particularly the construction of the beautiful bridge over the Bothenoth built in 1821 were extravagances that could ill be afforded. Plans were drawn up for additions to the house but in 1839 they had to be abandoned because, by then, debts were mounting to over £149,000. Luckily, the fine octagonal game larder built in the courtyard was completed before the money ran out. In his desperation and growing muddleheadedness the Viscount had borrowed money. Without their knowledge he pledged the surety of his son John, Master of Arbuthnott, his brother General the Honourable Hugh Arbuthnott of Hatton and his brother-in-law the Earl of Airlie by forging their signatures. In 1848 it was found that the eighth Viscount had obtained promissory notes to the value of £31,000 over a long period using his

*John, eighth Viscount of Arbuthnott, from a portrait by Sir David Wilkie funded by public subscription. He was nearly ruined by the cost of improvements to the estate, including the building of the bridge in the background, before a head injury and prosecution for forgery condemned him to a lonely death in exile.*

relatives' false guarantee. The family made good all the debts which had been made in their names when all this was discovered but it was too late to prevent a case being made against him for *"fraud, forgery and uttering"* and put before grand juries in Forfar, Stonehaven and Aberdeen, who were all directed to send his case for trial. This they did with great reluctance since his mental condition was well known.

> *Stonehaven Journal: August 22 1848 - The Arbuthnott Grand Jury took the unusual step of writing to the House of Lords stating that they felt the the Viscount had no dishonest intention, but acted under the influence of an unsound mind. There are many circumstances, perfectly well known in the district, and there are others currently reputed and believed, and are in part known to some of us to be true, all leading to the suspicion, not to say the conviction, that the insanity has been gradually advancing over many years, and had its origins in a fracture of the skull which his Lordship sustained in 1829, a portion of the frontal bone having been so completely destroyed that it was taken away. It was our wish..... that we were required to enquire further into these matters but the Clerk informed us that we might not so enquire and we followed his instructions. We feel however that it is due to our consciences, having*

*returned a True Bill, due to you as Public Accuser, and due to the Accused and his family to make this statement'. His Lordship's relatives are understood to have taken upon themselves the liquidation of his pecuniary liabilities, thus relieving his creditors from debt.*

The Viscount by then had left the country. Two years later, in a hotel room in Bruges, he signed papers handing over all his responsibilities to his son. It must be assumed that the Viscount never returned home. There is no record of his burial at Arbuthnott; his grave is unknown.

### The Years of Despondency

An aunt of the present Viscount said she once saw a sad lady in a long grey dress in the drawing room. It seems strange to recall these sad times in a house which has such a warm and happy atmosphere and this sighting was not typical of the experiences of others who have seen "*presences*" in the house. A quotation from a letter written by the present Viscount to a man who wrote to tell him of seeing a woman's figure silhouetted against the window as he woke in the early morning, may illustrate best the nearest thing to a ghost story that is ever likely to come from Arbuthnott House.

*I do not believe in the traditional ghost and I repeat that there are no traditional ghost stories attached to Arbuthnott House although a number of our more excitable friends and relations have tried to invent them. What I do believe however is that any old house with a continuous occupation by the same family, in this case for 800 years, must occasionally bring out of the past an atmosphere or feeling of, as I have called it, a 'presence' who invariably just seems to be interested in what is going on in the present day. For your interest my experience of this was as a young man about to join the Navy in the 1939-45 war when I had the clear impression of someone asking me what I was going to be doing during the war. On my reply that "I was going to join the Fleet Air Arm" all interest ceased and the 'presence', apparently satisfied, evaporated.*

The eighth Viscount had six sons and seven daughters. Of his daughters, two died young and the rest married. Of his sons, John the eldest inherited and remained at Arbuthnott, the second, Walter, after serving in the army, went to live at Hatton the home of his uncle, General Sir Hugh Arbuthnott. For the others there was no longer the old Arbuthnott tradition (at its height in the days of Robert, fourteenth Laird), of all the sons being provided with land. Now there was no money and they had to go out and help to build and maintain the Empire in the Victorian tradition. Hugh, great-grandfather of the present Viscount joined the Madras Light Cavalry and was at Lucknow during the Indian Mutiny, David entered the Madras Civil Service and Charles joined the Bengal Light Infantry. After serving in the army, William married the rich and twice-widowed Barbara Ferguson. After two summers spent in Norway, the couple parted. William returned to Scotland. Barbara chose to remain in Norway, where she stayed for the rest of her life, generous to the local people, she lived in great style and became known as 'The Uncrowned Queen of Sunndalen'.

### John, ninth Viscount and twenty-sixth Laird
### 1860-1891

John, ninth Viscount carried on managing the estate within the financial strictures which he inherited, having paid his father's debts as best he could. He was no doubt helped and supported by his uncle, 'the General', who was Member of Parliament for Kincardineshire from 1826-1864 and a well-known and respected figure in the district. There is a portrait of a young man holding a gun, thought to be the ninth Viscount. He was thus portrayed in a pose which he must have adopted almost daily, as did his sons, shooting being very much their main preoccupation. The eighth Viscount's game larder was much used and any available money was spent on guns.

In 1837 the ninth Viscount had married Lady Jean Ogilvy, daughter of the Earl of Airlie and his first cousin through his mother, Margaret Ogilvy. The union produced four sons, none of whom had children and three of whom were to become Viscount in turn.

His brother Hugh had died in India leaving two young sons, aged eight and six. Virtually penniless, the two boys were brought home to Scotland by their mother, Susannah Campbell, to be brought up in Edinburgh. Luckily for them growing up in such straitened circumstances, the boys were very intelligent, and the elder one, John and was among the first pupils at newly founded Fettes College in 1870. He was destined to be the father of the fifteenth Viscount. He wrote to his uncle, John, ninth Viscount to tell him that he had gained second place in his entry exams to the Indian Civil Service. His reply reveals the ninth Viscount as a kindly affectionate man with limited interests.

*Dec 28* [18]77

*My Dear John,*

*I got your letter this morning and send you enclosed a new year's gift, in the shape of check on Coutts for £140. I have no knowledge of such matters, but should think what you propose doing must be of advantage to you afterwards.*

*We have had very hard weather with some snow since Sunday, and this morning they are filling the icehouse, the glass showing 10 degrees of frost. Let me know that you get the enclosed all right.*

*The Hattons go to London next week I believe to be present at*

*Charlie's marriage, a foolish affair I think he might have done
much better - Remember me to you Mother and believe me
your affectionate Uncle
Arbuthnott
There are so many Arbuthnotts at Coutts now, that I have given
both our names on the check.*

The "*Hattons*" are his brother Walter and family, who lived at Hatton. His displeasure at the marriage of their son Walter Charles (Charlie), who was later to become the thirteenth Viscount, was probably that the bride was of the English landed gentry which may have seemed undesirable to a family who up to this point seem to have chosen their wives almost exclusively from the Scottish aristocracy. Further evidence of the snobbery innate in the nobles of Victorian Scotland and apparently displayed by the ninth Viscount comes from a family story which tells that when one son suggested that he go into business with a friend his father forbade him saying "*You might as well start a sweetie shop in Bervie*". He meant that people of their kind did not do such things. Narrow social rules dictated that the Law, the Church and the Army were the only careers deemed suitable for a gentleman.

When John, ninth Viscount died in 1891, Victoria could still look forward to another decade as Queen and Empress. The ninth Viscount was a typical Victorian gentleman in his love of sport, his sense of honour and his narrow views of class. He chose to be buried in the family aisle.

### John, tenth Viscount and twenty-seventh Laird
### 1891-1895

The four sons of the ninth Viscount all remained living in the house after his death. None of them achieved anything in life, perhaps because they were the children of first cousins or because they lacked a formal education.

The eldest son John, tenth Viscount, married but had no children. His wife, Harriet, must have led a strange life as the only woman in a household of four brothers. It was after his death that the Missal and other precious books and documents were sold in an attempt to raise cash. Canon Edmund Arbuthnott writes of an incident during his lifetime "*which originated with my Aunt Margaret, who stayed at Arbuthnott in the days of John* [10th Viscount]. *She said that Uncle John* [the Viscount] *thought so little of the Arbuthnott Missal as to keep it in a drawer with fishing tackle. She had the impression that he would give it to her had she asked*".

### David, eleventh Viscount and twenty-eighth Laird 1895-1912 and
### William, twelfth Viscount and twenty-ninth Laird 1912-1917

Two of his brothers David and William inherited the title in turn. The fourth brother, Hugh was an invalid who did not outlive his brothers. None of the brothers married or had children. By 1917 when the last brother, William, who had become a recluse, died, the house, garden and estate were in a state of total neglect and decay. Their heir was Walter Charles Warner Arbuthnott, usually known as Charlie, their first cousin.

The reminiscences of Dorothy Oxley, who was to become the wife of the fourteenth Viscount of Arbuthnott and which she wrote in 1960, give an idea of what life was like in the days before and during the 1914-18 War:

*The old laird* [the 12th Viscount] *had ceased to care and he was looked after by an old retainer, Preddy. Now Preddy was engaged when only a lad to attend to Mr Hugh, the invalid brother. He became absolutely devoted to his charge and to the family. Years went by and Mr Hugh died and Preddy in devoted remembrance kept his bedroom as if Hugh was to return. Preddy was a man now and soon became very much the confidential servant of his master the 12th Viscount. With his brothers dead and few friends the old laird lived a lonely life in one corner of the House. Preddy was his standby and comfort. Preddy became more and more indispensible. He knew everything and soon was in charge of everything. Doubtless he was treated very generously in every way by his master.*

*Preddy took over for himself the farm "The Deep" and managed to obtain one of the few tractors on the market then. Now Preddy was a farmer! so the Trustee put him in charge of the Home Farm. They did not realise in Edinburgh how inefficient and unreliable Preddy could be. Even during, or perhaps because of, the War, neighbouring farms made profits. Arbuthnott Home Farm was run at a loss.*

The situation at Arbuthnott had degenerated. Where once the laird and his immediate family lived in the house, surrounded by his relations living nearby, now a lonely old man sat disconsolately in one room of the house and allowed his butler to take over completely.

It was at this time that Lewis Grassic Gibbon, celebrated author of *Sunset Song*, *Cloud Howe* and *Grey Granite*, which evoke such a strong picture of local life in the early days of the twentieth century, grew up in the parish of Arbuthnott. It is little wonder that he wrote of the lairds of 'Kinraddie' with so little respect in his books. The fortunes of the family at Arbuthnott were at their nadir, the sons of the ninth Viscount did nothing but stay at home and shoot rabbits.

### Walter (Charlie), thirteenth Viscount and thirtieth Laird 1917-1920

The thirteenth Viscount was a first cousin, Walter 'Charlie' Warner Arbuthnott, who had lived in the south of France for many years because of his wife's health. He it was, whose marriage to Marion Parlby of Manadon in Devon had been so disapproved by the ninth Viscount. They had two sons, Jack, who was to inherit, and Robin, who was wounded in the First World War in 1915 and married his nurse, Kitty Lucas, and two daughters, Muriel and Nancy.

He came to Arbuthnott in 1917 in his sixties to find his entire inheritance derelict and heavily mortgaged. The sight that greeted his daughter Muriel when they first arrived was that of workmen trundling barrowloads of debris out of the second floor bedrooms and easing them down ramps that had been put down the main staircase. The family spent the summers in the uncomfortable house, where, despite her ill health, *"Marion didn't mind the rats"**. Walter only lived for three more years, however his son Jack was to live at Arbuthnott for the next forty years.

---

* From conversation with Mrs Hew Blair-Imrie, 1992

# Chapter 10

## The Years of Revival

*John (Jack), fourteenth Viscount and thirty-first Laird 1920-1960*
*"from log cabin to laird"*

When Jack, fourteenth Viscount inherited Arbuthnott, he and his wife were in Canada. He had emigrated fifteen years earlier in the early 1900s and started up a ranch from virgin ground. He then built a wooden house for his bride who joined him out there. This experience of pioneering ranch work stood Jack Arbuthnott in good stead when he had to build up the Home Farm at Arbuthnott after a long period of neglect and mismanagement. If we return to the reminiscences of Dorothy, Lady Arbuthnott, widow of the fourteenth Viscount, we can get a picture of the sad state of affairs that she and her husband found at Arbuthnott on their return from Canada to take up their inheritance in 1920. The house was heavily mortgaged and up for sale and it was only due to the efforts of Nick MacPhail the trustee and Mr Beveridge of the Edinburgh law firm, Lindsay Howe WS, that the house was saved for the family and did not join the hundreds of mansions in Scotland that were pulled down or sold after the First World War.

*In 1920 Arbuthnott lands stretched from Fordoun to Inverbervie but nearly all were heavily mortgaged and the creditors were pressing for their dues. Every farm, every hillside was up for sale. Even the Mansion House which for six [seven] centuries had only housed Arbuthnotts Even the Mansion House was up for sale. Farms and moors were taken over by other hands But the trustee was determined to save, if possible, the House and as many surrounding acres as could be rescued. The old House was in a sorry state, dilapidated, unpainted and dreary. Rats ran behind the panelled walls, water dripped from the cupola and large damp patches disfigured the walls of the inner hall. The gardens too had almost disappeared and the once well kept lawns now closely resembled a hay field.*

*However it was no time, nor was it the intention of the Trustee, to make either house or garden attractive. No amenities must be added to the house, rather let any would-be purchaser think the place beyond repair. So it happened, one or two come to inspect and turned away; "Too far gone". In even the long*

*neglected but infinately picturesque drive with its overhanging
trees and bushes and verges deep with the fallen leaves of many
years, even that did not tempt them.*

*There was little money to count on, for in seven years the Estate
had suffered from the loss of three lairds, three death duties and
three succession duties were a heavy burden on any estate and
in 1920 the Stock Exchange was very low too. It was Mr
Beveridge who suggested a gamble, borrow for death duties and
hope for a rise in the scanty shares. Luckily after a few months
the investments recovered and much money was saved.*

*Now to turn to the rest of the Property. Two thousand [in fact
three thousand] acres surrounding the family home were rescued from the Mortgagees. Tenants held Milltown, Pitcarles,
Townhead, Hercules Haugh and a croft or two, but the Home
Farm had been run by, or for the lairds for many years.*

*In 1920 this farm was in the same sorry state as the rest of the
policies. Partly owing to the depradations of the first World
War and partly, or perhaps mostly to mismanagement and
neglect. Years ago for the sake of sport the Bamph Hill had
been reserved as a rabbit warren and thousands of rabbits met
their death in this enclosed hillside. By 1920 no grass, but only
moss grew there. The wire was down and hungry rabbits
surged everywhere running wild over fields and even into the
neglected gardens.*

With the arrival of the fourteenth Viscount and his wife the desolate atmosphere at Arbuthnott became transformed. Since most of the land had been
sold, relations could no longer live in close proximity but after the initial strictures imposed while the estate was being redeemed from the mortgagors, life
and laughter returned to the place. Though sadly Jack, fourteenth Viscount and
his wife never had children of their own, the house and garden rang with the
sound of young voices and a happy and welcoming atmosphere prevailed.

By 1926 Jack, fourteenth Viscount, had taken up office as Lord-Lieutenant of
Kincardineshire, one he held until 1960.* He was also Convenor of
Kincardineshire County Council from 1935 to 1960 and held several other
important posts in north east Scotland. With his ranching experience in
Canada, he could use his skills in the task of making the Home Farm a viable
concern and bringing the remaining acres of woodland to order. Lady
Arbuthnott set about the task of restoring the third Viscount's garden at
Arbuthnott to its former glory. She was a gardener of great enthusiasm and
knowledge, and over the years she turned it into a rich and varied treasury of
plants.

---

*At the Coronation of Elizabeth II in 1953, he took the oath of allegiance on behalf of all
Viscounts.

*Jack, 14th Viscount of Arbuthnott, whose ranching skills stood him in good stead when he inherited Arbuthnott in a ruinous state after his father died unexpectedly of a heart attack in 1920. .*

*Dorothy (Dot) Oxley, wife of the 14th Viscount, who despite having no children of her own is still remembered for the happy children's parties she gave.*

The fourteenth Viscount died in 1960 when the title passed to his second cousin, Major-General Robert Keith Arbuthnott. His successor expressed the debt the family owed the fourteenth Viscount in a letter to his widow *"I have always had the greatest admiration for the way Jack and you laboured to restore the estate to its present fine condition ... and not only that but, between you, you restored the dignity of the family."*

### Robert Keith, fifteenth Viscount and thirty-second Laird 1960-1966 "the Soldier Laird"

Robert Keith Arbuthnott, fifteenth Viscount and thirty-second Laird, was born in 1897 in Assam, Northern India. He was grandson of the Hon. Hugh Arbuthnott, brother of the ninth Viscount, who had served in the Indian army during the Mutiny and died in 1866 when his sons, John and Hugh, were aged only eight and six. His widow, Susannah Campbell, returned to Edinburgh to bring up her sons on a very limited budget. After Fettes College, John entered the Bengal Civil Service in 1879 to start a distinguished career boosted by his uncle's cheque for £140. For many years he served as Deputy-Commissioner, later Commissioner, at Shillong in Assam, Northern India. He married Jeannie Hamilton, daughter of a merchant in the City of London, in 1887. By 1897 they had two daughters, Jeannie and Margaret and a son, Hugh and were expecting

109

another child. In June that year there was an earthquake in Assam which caused widespread devastation. *"Mr Arbuthnott, who with his wife and children had a very narrow escape, greatly distinguished himself by the prompt and vigorous measures he took to combat the terrible effects of the earthquake."* Two months later on 21 August, during another tremor, their fourth child, Robert Keith, was born in a tent in the garden where the family were sheltering while their bungalow was rebuilt. The baby was two months premature and thought unlikely to live. However, though small and never robust, he was to survive and fight in two world wars.

At six Robert was left in England with his elder brother to live with his uncle and aunt, Hugh and Daisy Arbuthnott. They already had a son called Robert, so from then on he was called Keith. During the time he was at school he only saw his parents and younger sister Susannah when they came home for the summer every three years. Before war was declared in 1914 his elder brother Hugh was already in the Indian Army, with the 69th Bengalis, stationed at Loralai, Baluchistan. Once war broke out, he spent two years defending the border against the Turks. In December 1915 the hospital in which Hugh lay wounded was overrun by Turkish troops. His body was never found. He became one of the many thousands with no known grave.

Keith was commissioned in the Black Watch when he was eighteen and shortly after was serving with the 1st Battalion in Flanders. In April 1918 his mother wrote to congratulate him on being awarded the Military Cross. By then he had been promoted and was commanding 'C' Company. He never received her letter, it was returned to her marked 'missing'. After waiting anxiously for news, his distraught parents heard through the Red Cross that their surviving son was wounded and in German hands. A tunnel being held by his company, with others, was over-run by the enemy, Keith who had been wounded early in the battle was captured lying in his company headquarters. There was little comfort in Room 31, Block III of the 'Offizieregefangenenlager' at Mainz in which he was held. One of the first cards his mother received from there read:

> *Dearest Oldie. I am quite well. Sorry I cannot write to you this week. I fancy you should have had word of me about a fortnight ago so I should get a letter in another fortnight. I have written to the Maple Dairy Copenhagen for butter and eggs and to the Red Cross there for bread. Hope you are well at home. There is no news to give you as there is very little doing here. Love to you all  Keith.*

Everyone was living in reduced circumstances at that stage of the war. The prisoners' diet consisted mostly of turnips. His family never heard this first hand from Keith, he never talked about the First World War.

After the war Keith served with the Black Watch in India. While on leave in

---

* From The Black and White Magazine, January 1898

1920 he became engaged to Ursula Collingwood, daughter of a family he had known since early childhood. Both Sir William Collingwood, his father-in-law and his uncle Hugh, with whom he lived while his parents were in India, worked for the Vulcan Foundry locomotive works. The young couple had to wait four years before they could marry since they were too young to be eligible for an army marriage allowance. Their wedding was in England on 10 January 1924, at Dedham Church, in Essex. Their eldest son, John Campbell, was born the following October at Dubton House, near Montrose in Scotland, the home of his paternal grandmother. They had two more sons, William David and Hugh Sinclair and a daughter, Christian Keith, named after the *"virtuous and worthy lady"* who married Robert, fourteenth Laird, in the late 1520s.

In 1936 Keith went to serve in Palestine where the Arab rebellion was at its height. There he commanded 'C' company in the 2nd Battalion of the Black Watch. His company was involved in action at Al Mughaiyir. In a letter sent to his mother in August 1938, Private R R H Shelmerdine wrote:

> *It was undoubtedly the most decisive action in Palestine, so far, and a great victory. Where the honours will go I cannot say. The Company Commander, Captain Arbuthnott set a brilliant example by his coolness and confidence*
> .

His official reward was the Distinguished Service Order, a more telling honour was the affectionate nickname 'Teddy' by which he was known to his Company.

After the outbreak of the Second World War he was appointed to command the 6th Battalion of the Black Watch which was deployed in the south of England to defend the country against the expected invasion by the Germans. After various other staff postings he was sent, in 1943, to Italy to command the 11th Infantry Brigade. This brigade was part of the 78th (or 'Battleaxe') Division within the 13th Corps, which in August 1944, came under the command of the American 5th Army under General Mark Clark. At that same time the 78th Division's Commander, Major-General Keightley, was promoted and a replacement was sent out from the U.K. The battle-weary troops were not able to accept a commander who had no front line experience. The uproar was such that the 13th Corps Commander, Lieutenant-General Kirkman, was obliged to accept the choice of the Brigadiers and allow command to be handed over *"to the senior of them, Arbuthnott. The latter's qualities were of course well known to Kirkman and were much in accord with his own. Both saw themselves as much protectors as commanders of their men. ... it is significant that Arbuthnott was confirmed in the appointment he had acquired through what amounted to a palace revolt and promoted GOC on November 27. A veteran of the Great War, aged 47, he would not have been accorded this honour if there had been any doubt in Alexander's mind about his division's fighting efficiency.* [Alexander was Commander-in-Chief in Italy.] *Arbuthnott had in fact steered 78th Division through a crisis brought about by conflict between the operational ambitions of Fifth Army and some unimaginative decisions by the Military Secretariat and Staff Duties Directorate. He was by no means the obvious choice for such a task, but he proved to be an inspired one. Unassuming, humane, quietly humorous, he completely lacked swagger and bluster, and indeed his slight, stooping figure would not have been identified as that of a soldier when seen out of uniform. Yet he was a shrewd tactician and knew the problems confronting junior officers from close observation of them. He made them feel that he was on their side, and this was the best contribution a general could make towards victory in the long test of endurance the Italian campaign had become."*

This account was given in Gregory Blaxland's *Alexander's Generals*. The conflict he describes arose from the American wish, personified in General Mark Clark, to end the war quickly, while veterans of the Great War, like Keith, who had witnessed the slaughter in the trenches, were unwilling to risk the lives of their men unnecessarily in a conflict which was inevitably going to end in victory. General Clark personally awarded Keith the American Legion of Honour during the Italian campaign.

At the end of the war the 78th Division became the army of occupation in Corinthia, Austria. This meant dealing with the tragic aftermath of the war, which involved refugee problems which were, even at that stage, compounded by the open hostility of our former allies, Russia and particularly Yugoslavia. The 'Iron Curtain' came down immediately across the border between Yugoslavia and Austria. In 1946, Keith was posted to Egypt, then to Edinburgh and he ended his army career as GOC the 51st Highland Division. Throughout his military career he had always been highly and affectionately regarded, particularly by his subordinates, as a first-rate regimental soldier. In 1960 he received the highest accolade in this respect when he was appointed Colonel of the Regiment.

When he was painted in 1958 in his uniform of Colonel of the Black Watch, he chose as the background, the silhouette of the *campanile* [bell tower] of the village of Cona near Ferrara, scene of the Battle of the Argenta Gap in April 1945. This he felt was the most decisive of the many battles fought by the 78th Division in the Italian campaign. In *Algiers to Austria: A History of the 78 Division in the Second World War*, Cyril Ray describes Major-General Arbuthnott's abilities at this point of the campaign:

*His ability to stage and fight infantry and tank attacks in quick succession by day and night, especially in the Argenta Gap fighting, was an achievement to be justly proud of. In this fighting in particular he showed how quick decisions by the commander combined with well trained gallant troops can achieve outstanding success if the enemy can be kept off his balance by a series of quick blows. The enemy was never really able to recover himself at this stage chiefly due to Keith Arbuthnott's skill and determination.*

*Major General Robert Keith Arbuthnott, who was to become the 15th Viscount, on campaign in Italy in 1944; "a much loved as well as a most successful commander".*

PHOTO COURTESY OF THE IMPERIAL WAR MUSEUM.

When Keith inherited the Viscountcy from his cousin Jack in 1960, and he and his wife, Ursula, went to live at Arbuthnott, they found the house, and especially the roof, needed urgent repair. The restrictions on building as a result of the war and his predecessor's failing health meant that nothing had been done to the house over recent years except the much-needed restoration of the drawing room ceiling which was undertaken with a grant from the Historic Buildings Council. He immediately set about extensive remedial work, which included the entire reconstruction of the roof. He also instigated the replanting of the first third of the renowned beech avenue. The strain of two wars had taken their toll however and he only lived at Arbuthnott for six years. He spent those years living with the inconvenience of building work and not even beginning to see the effect of the work which resulted in the house being in the beautiful condition in which it is today. The first laird to take an active interest in the kirk for many years, he became an elder. Once more the Laird and his wife worshipped at the Kirk of St. Ternan.

In 1962, the fifteenth Viscount and his wife were invited to Canada in his capacity as Colonel of the Black Watch. The Canadians asked for a sample of his tartan so that they could welcome him with the appropriate display. As a lowland family, the Arbuthnotts had no traditional pre-Culloden tartan and had not had one created in the Victorian period. With great presence of mind Robert Keith promised to have a tartan ready for the visit. A tartan was designed with the help of his wife and sons and registered in the Book of the Lord Lyon King of Arms in Scotland. The fifteenth Viscount, also asked the Lord Lyon to matriculate (re-register) the Laird's Coat of Arms, the first time this had been done since 1485 in the days of Robert, twelfth Laird* .

He could be said to have literally died with his boots on since he was wearing his uniform of Lord Lieutenant. Despite feeling unwell, he struggled to dress for a formal occasion with his wife at his side, but he collapsed and died of a heart attack. By his wish, his ashes and those of his wife, Ursula, are buried in the Arbuthnott Aisle.

Robert Keith, fifteenth Viscount held the view that the more one is given in life, the more one should give, a sense of the obligation and duty which ought to go with a position of authority. Although Laird for only six years, he had sufficient impact on both house and family at Arbuthnott to emulate Robert, twelfth Laird for whom he had a strong admiration.

### *John, sixteenth Viscount and thirty-third Laird 1966 -*

John Campbell Arbuthnott was born at Dubton House, by Montrose on 26 October 1924. A short time after his parents were married in January of that year, his father had returned to India where he was serving in the army. Soon after his birth, his mother took John out to India where he spent his early childhood. Like his father and grandfather before him he was educated at Fettes College, Edinburgh. Immediately on leaving school in 1942 he chose to go into the Royal Navy for his wartime service and entered the Fleet Air Arm as Naval Airman FX96040. He went to the United States of America for his flying training. On his return, while still only nineteen, he was drafted to join 849 Squadron on the aircraft carrier HMS Victorious in the Near East and the Pacific as the pilot of an Avenger. He was awarded the Distinguished Service Cross. The war in the Far East lasted until September 1945, when the Japanese finally surrendered.

At the end of the war John went to Cambridge University from where he graduated in Estate Management in 1949. That September he married Mary Oxley, whom he had known since childhood because she was a niece of Dorothy, wife of the fourteenth Viscount. They went to live in Yorkshire, where John worked for the Agricultural Land Service. A year later their son, John Keith Oxley Arbuthnott was born. Their daughter Susanna was born four years after that when the family had moved to Leicestershire. In 1955 they moved to Midlothian, when John started to work for the Nature Conservancy in Scotland as Land Agent.

In December 1966 his father, the fifteenth Viscount, died suddenly of a heart

---

* See Appendix 7 for extract from the registration of the Arbuthnott tartan and a description of the coat of arms.

*John, 16th Viscount and 33rd Laird with Pollaidh on the bridge at Arbuthnott in 1992*

attack and the following year John and his family moved into Arbuthnott House. At the time the parishes of Arbuthnott and Kinneff were being amalgamated, the minister chose to live in Kinneff, so the manse was no longer needed. It was bought by the estate and Ursula, the Dowager Viscountess moved there.

During the twenty-five years that they have been at Arbuthnott, the Laird and his wife have made constant improvements to the house and major repairs to eradicate dry rot. The most ambitious work has been the rationalisation of the back premises. A large family room, which serves as a cloakroom, gunroom and boiler room was built in place of a hotch-potch of old Victorian additions. Major reconstruction work also involved making a downstairs dining room in place of the old kitchen, with the pantry beside it being converted into the new kitchen. The house has been completely redecorated and all major public rooms and bedrooms re-carpeted. The cupola has been reglazed and all the plumbing modernised. The outside back premises have been re-organised into three garages, a stick house, coal shed and other outhouses. The entire area has been re-roofed and the backyard re-surfaced, while retaining the Victorian game larder. The house is now restored and adapted for the late twentieth century, when there are no longer several living-in servants, and, apart from help in cleaning the house, the Laird and his wife look after themselves.

The garden and associated grounds at Arbuthnott cover seventeen acres and are the particular province of the Laird's wife. With the help of two gardeners, Mary keeps it a show place that attracts many visitors when it is opened to the public. Her gift with flowers in their growing and her artistic flair in their arranging, are manifest in both the house and garden.

For a record of improvements to the estate the Laird himself can report: *"At the same time 400 acres of forest plantations were created and landscaped, and the Home Farm revitalised with new offices. Three new storage/cattle barns and a grain dryer were built. All estate cottages upgraded, west and main drives tarmacadamed, 200 acres of hill arablised and fenced. To pay for some of this and the death duties Townhead and Pitcarles farms were sold. Remaining farm boundaries for the Home Farm and Kirkton were replanned."* When John inherited as sixteenth Viscount there were still two impositions of death duty (inheritance tax) to pay.

From the time he came to live at Arbuthnott John became involved in many interests concerning the land and countryside in Scotland. He was a member of the Countryside Commission for Scotland from 1968-72, Chairman of the Red Deer Commission from 1968-74, President of the Royal Highland and Agricultural Society in 1975 and President of the Scottish Landowners Federation from 1974-79. He was Deputy Chairman of the Nature Conservancy Council from 1979-85. He was created Commander of the Order of the British Empire in 1986.

Following in the footsteps of previous lairds, he became the Lord Lieutenant (HM Queen's representative) of Grampian (Kincardineshire) Region in 1977 and sits in the House of Lords as a crossbencher with no affiliation to any one political party. He, also, like his predecessors, is involved in church activities, locally as an elder and treasurer at Arbuthnott Kirk and as Chairman of Kinneff Old Church Trustees and nationally as Chairman of the Scottish Churches Architectural Heritage Trust and Prior of Scotland of the Order of St John of Jerusalem, rekindling an interest in the Order which Robert, twelfth Laird held at the end of the fifteenth century.

*The Laird as the Lord High Commissioner to the General Assembly of the Church of Scotland with his Suite at the Palace of Holyroodhouse in 1987. (front) The Hon Mrs Bing, Lady-in-Waiting; John, 16th Viscount of Arbuthnott; the Viscountess of Arbuthnott; the Rev Ian Gough, Chaplain. (back) Flying Officer James Smart RAF, aide-de-camp; Miss Katie Mckenzie Stuart, Extra Lady-in-Waiting; Charles Fraser, Purse-bearer; Capt Tim Coles, Black Watch, aide-de-camp; the Hon Mrs Smith, Extra Lady-in-Waiting; Sub-Lieut. Gavin Don RN, aide-de-camp.*

In 1986 and 1987 he was appointed by the Queen as Lord High Commissioner to the General Assembly of the Church of Scotland. In this role he represented the Sovereign for the duration of the Assembly, taking up residence in the Palace of Holyroodhouse. The origin of the office dates back to the time of James VI who attended the General Assembly in person or appointed a Commissioner in his place, a practice which became essential when he inherited the English Crown and moved to London in 1603. The only monarch to attend the General Assembly since then is the present Queen. For the period that he holds the office, the Lord High Commissioner becomes the embodiment of the monarch, ranking next to the Queen and the Duke of Edinburgh and before the rest of the royal family. The Lord High Commissioner is addressed as 'Your Grace' as is his lady, the old Scottish term of address for the monarch, and the custom is for gentlemen to bow and for ladies to curtsey on first meeting them.  A Suite is appointed to attend their Graces and to assist in looking after the guests who are entertained at Holyrood during the week.  There are many public visits to hospitals, universities, and other institutions representing Scottish life.  Principal Arbuthnott would have approved of a laird of Arbuthnott being appointed to this office, also that the Church of Scotland still holds to the principle that the monarch is not the Head of the Church, as in England, but that the monarch's representative attends the Assembly by invitation and only as a witness, unable to vote or join in the debates.

The present Laird follows in the footsteps of his ancestors by taking part in the judiciary.  He is a Justice of the Peace and Chairman of the Kincardineshire and Deeside Justices Committee.  He has an active interest in education as a member of the Aberdeen University Court from 1978-84, as Patron of the Scottish Association of Geography Teachers and as President of the Royal Scottish Geographical Society from 1982-87.  His other Presidencies include that of the Royal Scottish Zoological Society and the British Association for Shooting and Conservation, a post from which he has only recently retired.  Among others, he holds directorships of the Clydesdale Bank, BP and the Scottish Widows Fund.

In 1986, John, sixteenth Viscount, handed over the running of the estate to his son and heir, Keith, who is styled 'The Master of Arbuthnott', a title held by the heir to any Scottish peerage that was created before the Act of Union in 1707.  Keith lives at the old manse, now called Kilternan, with his wife, Jilly Farquharson and children, Clare, Christopher and Rachel.

In 1977 the present Viscount and his wife founded the Arbuthnott Family Association, which has since spread worldwide.

On St Andrews Day, 30 November 1996, John, 16th Viscount was appointed a knight of the Most Ancient and Most Noble Order of the Thistle.*  This being the first time an Arbuthnott has been awarded this honour.  Each knight is appointed personally by the Queen.  Their number is limited to sixteen.

Members of the Family Association, wishing to commemorate this event, contributed to a pair of "Thistle Gates" which were unveiled in the garden at Arbuthnott during the 1997 Arbuthnott Gathering.

*See Appendix 8 on 'The Order of the Thistle'.

# Epilogue

While writing this story, I have been struck more and more with how much we are all inevitably children of our times. We cannot but be influenced by the events which surround us. This is never more true than in the case of the Lairds of Arbuthnott. An important factor in the continued occupancy of Arbuthnott has been their ability to adapt to those events. Did the first, second, third and fifth Viscounts each take an opposing ecclesiastical affliation through belief or because they wished to maintain their position? It is hard to say, but the first and fifth Viscounts were undoubtedly men of strong convictions. The latter certainly very nearly lost the estate and title because of them. If any chose to remain on their lands through compromise, I would like to think that their motive was to stay and look after the people for whom they were responsible. In the late nineteenth century, the occupants of the Big House forgot their duty to serve the community and the House of Arbuthnott very nearly failed. Then it would have been lost through apathy, which would have been far less forgivable.

So we come to the present time in this family saga. The question remains, why have the family managed to stay so long at Arbuthnott? Obviously, it has to be a combination of circumstances. One reason for the continued family occupation is the custom in the country of primogeniture. In the introduction to his sixteenth century history, Principal Arbuthnott mentions this factor:

> *It is evackit in ye lawes of our realme yat ye landis or barronies belonginge to houfis, fall not be divydit amage ye maill childeringe. Bet fall cum haill to ye eldest meallis onparited, for ye prefervinge of ye houfe.*

> *It is customary in the laws of our realm that lands and baronies belonging to a family, shall not be divided between the male children. But shall come to the eldest male undivided, in order to preserve the lineage.*

This custom has kept the lands together, the fact that the unbroken male line has been preserved must be ascribed to luck and the sensible choice of good motherly wives. However, in my judgement, the main reason that they have been kept in the family is that the Lairds have remained living on their lands, never at any time being absentee landlords. There has been a sound economic reason for this. The family has never owned any natural resources other than the land. Their wealth has come from that alone, and therefore they have had to remain in charge on their lands, though often handing on the responsibility of the day to day running of the estate to the heir.

But it goes deeper than this, anyone who lives at Arbuthnott finds that the place, the lands, the house and garden cast a spell. The charm is not always obvious, it is a cold and often bleak place to live even these days. It has never been coveted by anyone more powerful, as lands in a more mellow climate might have been and for this reason, those potential buyers who drove down the drive in the early 1920s to look at the place were not beguiled. They did not feel any special hold and left the family to resurrect the home built above the healing stream of Bothenoth that has housed them for over eight hundred years.

# Appendix 1
## The Origin of the Name.

The name Arbuthnott comes from the Celtic Aberbothenoth or Aberbuthenot. This word is derived from ABER, meaning the influx of a river into the sea or the joining of a smaller stream to a river, and BOTHENOT(H), which means little stream of virtue or healing power.

Surnames came into use during the thirteenth and fourteenth centuries, until then people had remained in small communities, where every individual was easily identified by one name. Then the population suddenly expanded and people moved for economic reasons to small townships and burghs and men began to be known by two names. There were three main sources for a second name, first and most obviously, a man could be called Donaldson or MacDonald after his father; alternatively he could be named Smith or Taylor because of his trade; or thirdly a man could be known by the name of the place from whence he came, as with Paisley, or as in the present case, Arbuthnott. Therefore everyone who has the surname Arbuthnot or Arbuthnott must have an ancestor who came from there.

There have been many variations on the spelling of Arbuthnot over the centuries, ranging from Arboythneth and Arbuthnotht to Arburthnet and many others. Today only two spellings are found, the difference being the inclusion or exclusion of the final "t", which shows a remarkable uniformity among later generations. The reason for this small variation may stem from the fact that, once spelling became a matter of importance, those members of the family who had moved from the area where the name originated kept to the form Arbuthnot, while those who remained within the immediate area, particularly the laird himself, used the same spelling as the place, Arbuthnott. Queen Victoria had an opinion on the matter. She remarked to her equerry, General Charles Arbuthnot, that she did not know why he did not spell his name with two "t"s, as Lord Arbuthnott did for she knew they were the same family with the same origins.

# *Appendix 2*

## Alexander Arbuthnott, printer, 1576-1585

Alexander Arbuthnot, a contemporary of Principal Alexander Arbuthnott, also made his name through the new religion. He was a descendant of the tenth Laird and his family had moved to Aberdeenshire. He had interests in both Aberdeen and in Edinburgh, where he was a burgher. He took up the hazardous trade of printing, which was then in its infancy in Scotland. Printers ran the danger of prosecution and imprisonment if those in power disapproved of the material produced.

Alexander went into partnership with Thomas Bassendyne, who had earlier been in trouble with the General Assembly. The Church leaders objected to a book called *The Fall of the Roman Kirk*, also an edition of psalms (said to include a bawdy song), that Bassendyne had printed. Under their orders it was Principal Arbuthnott who had examined and condemned them. By 1576 the authorities were needing to have Bibles printed, so it may not have been entirely a coincidence that Bassendyne and Arbuthnot became partners. If Principal Arbuthnott (by then an ex-Moderator of the General Assembly and to be elected twice more) was looking for a reliable person to assist Thomas Bassendyne, the only man in Scotland with the expertise to use a printing press, who better than his cousin and namesake.

On June 30th 1576 Bassendyne and Arbuthnot became the King's printers. They received a licence, under the Privy Seal, to print the Bible. This was to be the first printing in Scotland and in the vernacular (everyday language), therefore the first time that the Bible became available to the general public. The New Testament was printed in 1576, but then Bassendyne died and, as there were no Scotsmen trained to operate a printing press, Alexander had to employ a Flemish printer. This man called Salamon Kirknet of Madeburgh was paid 49 shillings a week, a princely sum for those days. The Bible was completed by 1579. The licence had given the printers a monopoly on the sale of the Bible and every "*substantial*" householder was obliged to buy one. This would have seemed to be a source of great prosperity but Alexander ran into difficulties. So many men, anxious to do right by owning a Bible, sent him money and orders that he found it impossible to print enough to meet their demands. So, in turn, he was faced with writs because of non-delivery. He died in 1585 with his family inheriting his financial problems.

# Appendix 3

## The Poems of
## Principal Alexander Arbuthnott, 1538-1583

Under my god, I would obey my prince,
But civil war does so trouble the cause,
That scarcely do I know  whom to reverence,
What to avoid, or what to embrace,
Our nobles now so fickle are, alas!
This day they say, (that which) tomorrow they will repent,
Is it surprising that I mourn and lament?

Gladly would I live in concord, and in peace;
Without division, rancour or debate.
But now, alas! in every land and place
The fire of hatred kindled is so hot,
That charity rings in no estate;
But all concur to hurt the innocent.
Is it surprising that I mourn and lament?

I love justice and wish that every man
Had that which rightly does to him belong;
Yet all my kin, allies, or my clan,
In right or wrong I must always support,
I must applaud, when they their interests show,
Though conscience thereto does not agree,
Is it surprising that I mourn and lament?


Extract from *The Praises of Women*

Obedient to her man
Just like a willow branch,
Both faithful and ardent
Always ready to follow commands.

# Appendix 4

## Letter from George, Master of Marshal to the Laird of Arbuthnott, 1580

*Rycht honorabill and weil belouit Cousing,*
*I have onderstand be this bearer that, at by rqueist, ye ar will-*
*ing your eldest sone suld spend a pairt off his tyme in my com-*
*pany, qyhairinto I think myself oblist unto yow, assurand yow*
*that he sall be no oder wayis vsit and tratit thane my selff, and*
*sall alik nathing that may be ffor his fordrance that lyis in my*
*power. Fairdermoir, the minister, our cousing*, schew me that*
*ye wald haue knawin in quhat equipage, concernyng his*
*horssis, seruantis, and claiss, it was meit he suld be. My opin-*
*ion is, that he will nocht mistar ony servants, in respect myne*
*sall haue that command to weit upon him; also, as concernyng*
*his horsis, indeid I think he will mister tway, in respect of the*
*kingis grace saylie ryding, quhairat baith I and he man contin-*
*uallie be present; as to his manner of clething, in that he may*
*haue his awin fre will; yit, seing he will be estemed as off my*
*company, I think it will nocht be on meit to be in blak, bot in*
*all thais ye sall do as you think guid. I haue schawin by opin-*
*ion onlie becauss I was requered off it. I supppone that I sall*
*nocht gang to the court quhyll efter by Lord Marris brydell,*
*quhilk will be in the end off this moneth, so that in the mem*
*tyme, giff ye and he thinkis guid, he may cumouer heir and*
*pass the tyme in huntying, or ony oder pastyme as sall occurre.*
*So nocht wylling to truble yow with farder letter, bot with my*
*hartlie commendation to your bedfellow and sonnis; quhome,*
*and yow, I commit to the protection of the Almychty, our guid*
*God. From Dunotter, this xxii off October, 1580, be*

> *Your assured guid Freind,*
> *Mastir Marschall*

*To the rycht honorabill and weill belouit cousing, the*
*Laird of Arbuthnot, delyer this.*

Right honourable and well beloved cousin, I have understood from the bearer of this letter that, at my request you are willing that your eldest son should spend part of his time in my company, wherein I think myself obliged to you, assuring you that he shall be in no other way used and treated than myself, and shall lack nothing that may be for his comfort that lies in my power. Furthermore, the minister, our cousin*, told me that you would like to know what he will need in the way of horses, servants, and clothes. I feel that he will not need any servants, because mine will be instructed to look after him. As far as horses are concerned I think he should have two because the King's grace (His Majesty) rides daily, when both I and he will always be expected to be present; as to the sort of clothes that he will need, he can please himself as far as that is concerned, although as he will be considered on an equal footing with me, I do not think that black would be appropriate, however you must do as you think fit. I am only giving my opinion because you asked me for it. I don't think that I will go to the court until after Lord Mars' wedding, which is to be at the end of this month, so that in the meantime, if you both think it a good idea, he may come over here and pass the time in hunting, or any other pastime which may be going on. So as I don't want to bother you with another letter, but with my best regards to your wife and sons, who, and you, I commit to the protection of the Almighty, our good God. From Dunnottar, this 22 October 1580.

Your very good friend,
Master of Marshal

Please deliver to my right honourable and well beloved cousin, The Laird of Arbuthnott

---

\* The minister at Arbuthnott Kirk, Robert Arbuthnott, was a cousin to both boys being the fourth son of Robert, fourteenth Laird and his wife, Lady Christian Keith.

# Appendix 5
## Letter from King James VI to Andrew, 15th Laird requesting supplies against the arrival of his Queen, 1589

*Richt traist freind, we greit yow weill.*

*Our mariage now, at Godly pleasour, being concludit, and the Quene our bedfellow hourlie louked for to arrive, it becummis ws to haue sic as accumpanies hir weill and honorablie interteinet, as our ambassadoure hes fund the lyk in pruif already. To the furtherance quhairof, we mon employ the gudewill of our loving subiectis, of best affectioun and habilitie, and thairfor eirnistlie and effectwuslie desyris yow that ye will send hither to the help of the honorable charges to be maid in this actioun, sic quantitie of fatt beif and muttoun, on futt, vyld foullis, and venysoun, or vther stuff, meitt for this purpois, as possible ye may provide and furneueis of your awin, or be your moyane, and expeid the samyn heir with all diligence, efter the ressait of this our letter, and delyuer ot to our seruitour, Walter Neasch, master of our lairdner, quhome we haue appoyntit to ressaue the samyn, and gif his ticket thairvpon. That we may particularlie knaw the gude wilis of all men, and acknawledge it accordinglie, quhen tyme servis; and that ye delyuer your ticket of that quhilk ye send, to ane of our master househaldis, quha sall attend thairvpoun, aduertising him quhat salbe lipnit for, that we be nocht dissappointit; as ye will do ws richt acceptable pleasour and service. And sa for the present committis yow to God.*

*At Edinburght, the penult day of August 1589.*

*James R*

*To our right traist freind, the Laird of Arbuthnot.*

Greetings our dear trusted friend.  Now that our marriage has been concluded with God's blessing, and that we daily expect the arrival of the Queen our bedfellow, it is appropriate that we should entertain her honourably and well in the manner which our ambassador has already found to be suitable.  To this end we must make use of the generosity of those loving subjects who are most able to support us, therefore we earnestly and decisively urge you to send here to help towards the furtherance of this task, such quantities of fat beef and mutton, on foot, wild fowl, and venison, or other provisions suitable for this purpose, either by providing them yourself, or if not, by obtaining them elsewhere, and send them here as quickly as possible after receiving this letter to our servitor, Walter Neasch, master of our larder, whom we have appointed to receive them and to give a receipt. In order that we may particularly know the goodwill of all men and acknowledge it accordingly, when the occasion arises, we ask you to show your receipt for that which you send to one of our master householders, who will act upon it, you should tell him about those provisions you are responsible for so that we may not be disappointed; this service will please us greatly. As for the present we commit you to God. At Edinburgh, the penultimate day of August 1589.

James R

To our dear and trusted friend the Laird of Arbuthnott.

# Appendix 6
## The Family of the Rev. Alexander

The fortunes of the family of the Rev. Alexander Arbuthnot will serve well as an illustration of how members of the family, during the eighteenth century, moved much further afield, at first keeping their bonds of kinship, and then gradually losing contact with their homeland.

All the sons of the Reverend Alexander Arbuthnot moved away from Scotland. John, the eldest, to fame if not fortune, in London. He was trained in medicine at St Andrews and became physician to Queen Anne. He was a close friend of Alexander Pope and moved in the same circles as such literati as Dean Swift and Samuel Johnson. In 1712 he published a series of pamphlets advocating the end of the war with France, *The History of John Bull*, in which Britain was satirized as John Bull *"an honest plain-dealing fellow, choleric, bold, and of a very inconstant temper"* who came to typify the national character. James Boswell records a conversation with Dr Johnson *"We talked of the geniuses in England in Queen Anne's reign. Mr Johnson said he thought Dr. Arbuthnott the first man among them: as he was the most universal genius, being an excellent physician, a man of deep learning and also great humour"*.

John's brother Robert, who had fought at the battle of Killiecrankie for the Stuart cause, went to Rouen in France and established the firm of 'Arbuthnot et Cie', Bankers. In later life he moved to Paris, where he kept up his Jacobite activities and gave shelter to many, including those who had had to flee from Scotland to France after the failure of the 1715 rising.

Another brother, Alexander, went to India. The youngest, George, settled in London and became a member of the Queen's Guard. However when Queen Anne died in 1714 and the crown went to the Hanoverian line, George felt he could no longer serve the monarchy and emigrated to France, where he also took part in Jacobite activities. Finally he decided to go to China, where he died, leaving a young son, John. This John, after trying various ventures in England and France, was offered the post of Inspector-General to the Irish Linen Trade in 1782. The appointment took him to Ireland where he decided to settle, buying land at Rockfleet in County Mayo. He married five times and had eleven children. His eldest two sons went to India , the third, Charles, later became Ambassador to Turkey. Charles and his wife were close friends of the first Duke of Wellington. In Charles' later years, when both he and the Duke were widowers, he became the constant companion and only close confidant of the 'Iron Duke'. His son, General Charles Arbuthnot, was equerry to Queen Victoria. It was to him that the Queen made her remark concerning the spelling of the family name.

The fourth son of John of Rockfleet became Bishop of Killaloe, the fifth and sixth became distinguished generals.

# Appendix 7

## The Tartan

Wit ye me that in the exercise of the power competent to and vested in me as Viscount of Arbuthnott and Chief of the Name and Arms of Arbuthnott, I have ordered and appointed likeas I now order and appoint that the proper tartan of my said Clan Arbuthnott is and shall be of the colours and proportions hereinafter specified videlicet:

*8 blue (pivot); 2 black; 2 blue; 2 black; 2 blue; 8 black; 4 green; 2 white; 4 green; 4 blue; 4 green; 2 white; 4 green; 8 black; 10 blue; 2 black; 2 blue (centre pivot)*

And I consent to the registration of these presents in the Books of the Lord Lyon King of Arms in Scotland.
Dated 8 September 1962

## The Coat of Arms

The Viscount of Arbuthnott has, as his personal crest, a peacock's head. The motto is *"Laus Deo"* Praise be to God. His coat of arms consists of three mullets (five-pointed stars) and a crescent, all coloured argent (silver) on a field or background of azure (pale blue). Any member of the family may use the crest as a badge, but only if it is worn surrounded by a belt and buckle.

APPENDICES

# Appendix 8

## The Order of the Thistle

On 30 November 1996, the 16th Viscount of Arbuthnott became a member, or knight, of the Most Ancient and Most Noble Order of the Thistle.

James VII created the Order in 1687, principally to reward Scottish noblemen who supported his cause, and to help secure the King's religious influence at Holyroodhouse. The scheme perished during the "Glorious Revolution" of the following year. James and a few of the original knights fled to France, where the Jacobite branch survived until the death of the Cardinal Duke of York (brother of Bonnie Prince Charlie) in 1807. The Cardinal's Thistle jewel in now preserved with the Honours of Scotland in Edinburgh Castle.

In 1703 Queen Anne, motivated by Union politics rather than religion, revived her father's Order. She provided the basis for the present constitution, comprising the sovereign and 12 knights (increased to 16 in 1833). For more than 200 years the Thistle operated as an integral part of the patronage system, and most candidates were selected on the basis of their rank or service to the government rather than personal achievement. This changed in 1946, when the political parties agreed to relinquish control to the sovereign. It is now the personal appointment of the Queen.

Membership of the Order has mainly been confined to Scottish peers; it has also welcomed others, including King Olav V of Norway and Robert Menzies, the Australian Prime Minister, but only two women, the first one being Queen Elizabeth, the Queen Mother, in 1937. The earliest royal knight, Prince William, later (William IV) was nominated in 1770, when he was 4 years old. The Dukes of Edinburgh and Rothesay (Prince Charles) now wear the insignia. The organisation has weathered various changes since Queen Anne's revival, including the Jacobite risings that diminished the supply of Scottish peers. It has suffered only one expulsion, with the removal of the Earl of Mar after the Battle of Sherriffmuir in 1715 and the defeat of the first Jacobite rising.

Since 1972, knights have normally been appointed on St Andrew's day and presented with their insignia shortly afterwards. The knight's formal insignia consist of a green mantle, black hat and gold chain and a badge bearing the image of St Andrew. At other times they wear a silver breast star containing a thistle and the Order's motto (nemo me impune lacessit - no one provokes me with impunity), and a gold St Andrew badge suspended from a green sash.

Lord Arbuthnott was knighted and invested by the Queen at Buckingham Palace on 14 February 1997, and on July 14 he was installed by the Queen at a ceremony, attended by all the knights, in the Thistle Chapel at St Giles' Cathedral, Edinburgh. The original Thistle Chapel at Holyrood fell into ruin after 1688, and it was not until 1911 that a new spiritual home was inaugurated at St Giles' Cathedral. The present building houses the heraldic plates of the modern knights, while the ante-chapel contains a record of the knights from 1687 to 1910 and a memorial to the Earls of Leven who encouraged its construction and provided the necessary funds. The Chapel's decoration is dominated by the heraldry of the Edwardian knights, rendered in stone and glass throughout the building. The roof bosses commemorate the original knights of James VII and Anne, while a holy table was unveiled in 1943 to the memory of King George V, and a tablet in the floor was dedicated by the Queen in 1962 to her father's memory.

A banner bearing Lord Arbuthnott's arms is in St Giles' and his crest (a peacock's head) is set above a stall in the Chapel, where they remain during his lifetime. An armorial stall plate will also form a permanent testament to the special honour the Viscount received in 1996, when he joined one of the country's pre-eminent royal institutions, providing an important link between the Stewart sovereigns of the late 17th century and the current Scottish nobility.

With acknowledgement to Russell Malloch

# Glossary

The following terms may be unfamiliar to the reader, some are old Scots, some Scots words in current usage, others are legal or technical terms.

| | |
|---|---|
| -ton, -toun, -town | small village, hamlet |
| Aber | at the confluence of (often of the sea but also of two rivers) |
| Agnate | one who is descended from same male ancestor, esp by direct male line |
| Anent | with reference to, concerning, against, opposite |
| Bard | celtic strolling musician or minstrel |
| Bigging | building(s) |
| Boll | volume measure of grain or meal, 1 boll equivalent to 4 bushels (approx. 150 litres). |
| Bothenoth | holy stream with healing powers, literally 'little one of virtue' |
| Brieve | letter of authority |
| Broken | applied to a man outlawed for some crime or to one who had no feudal protector and had taken to a lawless life |
| Burgh (of barony) | burgh with right to trade locally |
| Burgh (royal) | burgh with right to trade abroad |
| Burn | stream |
| Covenanter | opposer of episcopal worship, protagonist of presbyterianism |
| Craw | Crow |
| Croft | smallholding, farmhouse on a small holding |
| Croill | chest or trunk |
| Depone/deponent | testify/witness |
| Factor | land agent, steward |
| fl. | floruit/ he flourished |
| Forester | officer in charge of a forest |
| Fractionement | right to a portion of the rent, usually afforded to dependents |
| Hagbut, hackbut | an early form of portable firearm |
| Heritor | one who inherits |
| Ilk | same, the same place |
| Imprimis | at first, firstly |
| In-(followed by a placename) | resident or tenant |
| Inver | on the banks |
| Jacobite | supporter of James VII and II (from Latin 'Jacobus') against William and Mary |
| Jointure | provision made for widow in husband's will |
| Kirk | church |
| Kirkto(u)n | group of buildings round kirk |
| Laird | lord, landowner, squire |

132

| | |
|---|---|
| **Lifts** | luggage |
| **Loch** | lake |
| **LoP** | lordship |
| **Missal** | book containing service of mass for a whole year |
| **Mormaer** | celtic noble holding lands directly from the King |
| **Multure** | fee paid to miller |
| **Muniment** | written record |
| **New Model Army** | name given to Parliamentary army, trained by Cromwell. |
| **Neyf, nativus** | serf |
| **Nyt, knoit** | a large part, a portion |
| **Pistolet** | a small firearm, early form of pistol |
| **Pleuchis** | area of land, approximately 13 acres |
| **Psalter** | book of psalms |
| **Put to the horn** | outlawed, proclaimed by a blast on a horn from the Mercat Cross in Edinburgh |
| **Quartermaster** | regimental officer with duty of assigning quarters, looking after rations etc |
| **Quihilk, qlk** | which |
| **Reeking** | smoking |
| **Roundhead** | soldier of Cromwell's parliamentarian army |
| **Serf** | tenant with no rights, slave |
| **Sheriff** | chief executive officer of Crown in county |
| **Steading** | farm buildings, farmstead |
| **Tack** | lease, tenancy |
| **Taking the cross** | to make a vow to fight in the Holy Land from which only the Pope could effect release |
| **Teind** | tenth part of income (usually in kind) owed for support of Church |
| **Terce** | right of widow to the liferent of one third of her husband's heritable estate |
| **Thane** | celtic noble holding lands from a mormaer and thence from the King |
| **Thrawn** | stubborn |
| **Tolbuith** | tolbooth, townhall, jail |
| **Vikings** | norsemen |
| **Wadset** | conveyance of land in pledge for debt with reserve power for the debtor to recover his lands of payment of the debt |
| **Wapinshaw** | periodic muster of men under arms in particular district |

# Bibliography

## Secondary Sources

A Concise History of Scotland by Fitzroy Maclean. Penguin.
A History of Scotland by J D Mackie. Allen Lane 1978.
A History of Scotland by Rosalind Mitchison. Routledge 1990.
A History of the Scottish People by T.C Smout. Fontana Press 1987.
Alexander's Generals by Gregory Blaxland. William Kimber 1979.
Algiers to Austria: A History of the 78 Division in the Second World War by Cyril Ray. Eyre & Spottiswoode 1952.
Arbuthnott by George Clark Suttie. James Bruce, Stonehaven 1992.
Arbuthnott House, Kincardineshire by Harry Gordon Slade. Proceedings of the Society of Scottish Antiquities Vol 110, 1978-80.
Celtic, Mediaeval Religious Houses in Angus by D G Adams. Chanonry Press Brechin 1984.
Domestic Annals of Scotland by Robert Chambers.
Ecological History of Angus by H A P Ingram.
Feudalism in Scotland by G.W.S.Barrow.
Kingship and Unity by G.W.S.Barrow. Edward Arnold 1981.
Memorials of Angus and the Mearns compiled by Andrew Jervise. David Douglas, Edinburgh 1885.
Memories of the Arbuthnots of Kincardineshire and Aberdeenshire by Mrs P S-M Arbuthnot. Allen & Unwin 1920.
Powerful Pots, Beakers in North-East History by Ian A G Shepherd. 1986.
Scotland, A Concise History BC to 1990 by James Halliday. Gordon Wright.
The Fraser Papers (Sir William Fraser's papers) edited by J.R.N.McPhail, KC University Press, Edinburgh 1924.
The Kirk of St. Ternan, Arbuthnott by George A. Henderson. Oliver & Boyd 1962.
The Lairds of Dun by Violet Jacob. John Murray 1931.
The Miscellany of the Spalding Club (vols. II & V) edited by J Stuart William Bennet, Aberdeen 1852.
The Normans in Scotland by R L G Ritchie.
The Scots Peerage edited by Sir J B Paul Edinburgh 1902.
Who's Who in Scottish History compiled by Gordon Donaldson & Robert S Morpeth. Basil Blackwell 1973.

## Primary Sources

The Arbuthnott papers Kings College Library, Aberdeen.